Twayne's English Authors Series

Sylvia E. Bowman, *Editor*

INDIANA UNIVERSITY

William Henry Hudson

 130

William Henry Hudson

By JOHN T. FREDERICK

Twayne Publishers, Inc.   ::   New York

Copyright © 1972 by Twayne Publishers, Inc.

All Rights Reserved

Library of Congress Catalog Card Number: 73-161817

MANUFACTURED IN THE UNITED STATES OF AMERICA

For Lucy

Preface

On a winter afternoon some forty years ago, I was in the university library looking for a book to read aloud to my two young sons—something which would interest both them and me. I took from the shelf W. H. Hudson's *The Book of a Naturalist,* read a few pages, and carried it home. The name of Hudson was known to me: I had read shortly after its appearance in 1924 Ford Madox Ford's *Joseph Conrad: A Personal Remembrance,* because of my already matured admiration for Conrad; and remembered his vivid description of Hudson's first visit to the farm where Conrad and Ford were collaborating on a manuscript: the "extremely tall man with a disproportionately small, grave head . . . in a pepper and salt gamekeeper's coat with tails, stalking past the window, examining the house with suspicion."[1] I remembered, too, Ford's assertion: "Our greatest admiration for a stylist in any language was given to W. H. Hudson of whom Conrad said that his writing was like the grass that the good God made to grow and when it was there you could not tell how it came."[2] But I had somehow missed *Green Mansions* in the period of its great vogue in the United States during the preceding decade; and I had read nothing else of Hudson's.

My choice was a happy one: both the boys and I were enchanted. I found Ford's and Conrad's admiration for Hudson's style fully confirmed by reading aloud (the only sure test for style). We read more of Hudson that winter, and I have ever since continued to read and reread as time permitted.

In general, the organization of the present study follows the chronological pattern of the composition of Hudson's works. An exception is my treatment of one of his last books, the wholly autobiographical *Far Away and Long Ago,* immediately after my sketch of his life because of the warm and bright light which it throws on the events of his early years.

Furthermore, I have felt it advantageous to treat the whole body of Hudson's fiction, from his first book—*The Purple Land That England Lost* (1885) to one of the last, *Dead Man's Plack and An Old Thorn* (1920)—in one section of the study rather than to disperse the half dozen books of fiction in a general chronological pattern. Finally, I believe that the reader's grasp of Hudson's achievement as an essayist, which is his greatest, may be facilitated by looking at the essays in groups identified by intention and by emphasis in subject matter rather than wholly by date of publication in book form.

To this end, I have arranged the volumes of essays in four groups: first, those primarily scientific in character; second, those devoted almost exclusively to birds, in observation and anecdote; third, those primarily marked by general presentation of the life of a specific region of England, with emphasis on human beings; and, fourth, those identifiable by their primary attention to matters of reflection and speculation, based on observation. This procedure gains further justification from the fact that most of the volumes of essays present in part, or entirely, items previously published as magazine articles, often many years before their appearance in book form.

Preparation of this book, involving the rereading and study of the whole body of Hudson's work and all I could find in print about him, has been a sustained pleasure and an intrinsic reward. My chief hope for the book is that it may lead others to the discovery, or rediscovery, of the range, the richness, and the significance of Hudson's work.

I wish to include in this Preface an expression of my sincere thanks to E. P. Dutton & Co., Inc., publishers in the United States of nearly all of the writings of W. H. Hudson, for permission to quote freely from his books published by them. I have done so extensively, in the conviction that Hudson is his own best interpreter and advocate.

I am grateful to Miss N. Willson and to The Society of Authors for permission to quote freely from the books of W. H. Hudson which are still under copyright in Great Britain, also to The Royal Society for the Protection of Birds.

JOHN T. FREDERICK

Contents

Chronology

1841   William Henry Hudson, born August 4; third son and fourth child of Daniel and Caroline Kimble, at "The House of the Twenty-five Ombú Trees," in the area of Quilmes, Argentina, a few miles from Buenos Aires.

1846   Family moved to "The Acacias," where the father operated a country store.

1857   Read Gilbert White's *Natural History of Selborne*. Father's business failure compelled return to "The Twenty-five Ombú Trees."

1858   Suffered a sustained attack of typhus, contracted on a visit to Buenos Aires, followed by an attack of rheumatic fever, caused by exposure, which threatened his life and left him with a permanently damaged heart.

1859   Mother died. Read Darwin's *The Origin of Species*.

1866   September 5, wrote to Dr. Spencer Fullerton Baird, assistant secretary of the Smithsonian Institution, offering to collect birdskins for the institution. Served for several months in the Argentinian army during the war with Paraguay. Collections acknowledged with honor in Smithsonian Reports.

1868   Father died. Sent bird collections to Dr. P. L. Sclater for London Zoological Society.

1870   First published work on Argentinian birds appeared in the form of letters to Dr. P. L. Sclater, in the *Proceedings of the Zoological Society of London*. The first letter was dated at Buenos Aires on December 14, 1869.

1871   Spent most of year in Patagonia.

1874   April 1, sailed for England.

1877   Married Emily Wingrave.

1880   Met Morley Roberts. Began writing for magazines.

1883   First story published, "Pelino Viera's Conversion."

1885   *The Purple Land.*

1886   Moved to a house in Westbourne Park, London, inherited by his wife, which became Hudson's home for the rest of his life, except for his frequent excursions to various parts of England.

1887   *A Crystal Age.*

1888   *Argentine Ornithology,* with P. L. Sclater. Hudson contributed the text on appearance, life, song, and habits; Sclater, the scientific descriptions.

1892   *The Naturalist in La Plata. Fan* (published under the pseudonym of Henry Harford).

1893   *Idle Days in Patagonia.*

1895   *British Birds.* Began active agitation for preservation of British bird life, resulting in formation of the Society for the Protection of Birds.

1898   *Birds in London.*

1900   *Nature in Downland.* Became naturalized British citizen. Awarded a civil list pension of 150 pounds a year, on recommendation of Lord Grey.

1901   *Birds and Man.*

1902   Met Edward Garnett. *El Ombú.*

1903   *Hampshire Days.*

1904   *Green Mansions.* Revision of *The Purple Land.*

1905   *A Little Boy Lost.*

1908   *The Land's End.*

1909   *Afoot in England.*

1910   *A Shepherd's Life.*

1911   Emily became ill.

1913   *Adventures Among Birds.*

1914   Emily bedridden; placed in guesthouse with nurse.

1916   Hudson ill in Cornwall. Began *Far Away and Long Ago.*

1918   *Far Away and Long Ago.*

1919   *Birds in Town and Village. The Book of a Naturalist.*

1920   *Birds of La Plata. Dead Man's Plack and An Old Thorn.*

1921   Emily Hudson died. *A Traveller in Little Things.*

1922   Died August 18, 1922. *A Hind in Richmond Park.*

CHAPTER 1

Life and Times

WILLIAM Henry Hudson was born August 4, 1841, at the *estancia* known as "The Twenty-five Ombú Trees," some ten miles from the then small city of Buenos Aires in Argentina. His parents had come to Argentina from New England to seek a climate beneficial to the father's health—he had been threatened by the "New England disease" of the times, tuberculosis—and also to search for a profitable investment. Land was cheap in Argentina: the tract acquired by Daniel Hudson in 1837 contained some four square miles. The presence of a considerable number of English settlers and land speculators in Argentina at this time—as well as English "remittance men" and others exiled or self-exiled to that country for various reasons—may have attracted Daniel Hudson. His father had been born and had grown up in England, and the sense of his English ancestry was strong in the American-born Daniel, though his mother was Irish. The early influence of this attitude helped to make W. H. Hudson feel at home in England in later years. His mother, however, was of American stock for generations; one of her ancestors had arrived on the *Mayflower*.

William was the fourth child and third son in a family of children that ultimately numbered seven, all born in Argentina. He was seven years younger than the firstborn brother, Daniel, and five years younger than the second son, Edwin. It would be impossible to overemphasize the importance of the place and the times in which Hudson spent his boyhood and youth in relation to his work as a writer. The traces of this early experience are found throughout his entire work, and it constitutes the whole material of one of his finest books, the autobiographical *Far Away and Long Ago*, written late in his life.

The farmhouse, already old when the Hudsons acquired the place, with its grove of great trees and the quiet stream nearby— and above all the great plains of the pampas itself—very early became, and remained, Hudson's greatest emotional possession. And there were the people: a few Englishmen, ranchers or exiles; a few descendants of old Spanish families; the majority gauchos, a few owners of small ranches, most employed on the lands of others. These were people of mixed blood, Indian and Spanish and some of Negro ancestry: skilled in their difficult and dangerous work of dealing with horses, cattle, and sheep; wholly illiterate; and violent, capable of enduring loves and hates, and careless of life. All of these characters, in rich variety, are encountered in *Far Away and Long Ago* as well as in some of Hudson's fiction.

When the future writer was six, his father purchased a larger establishment, "The Acacias," some fifty miles from Buenos Aires, where he moved with his family. This undertaking included the keeping of a rural store and dealing in hides, tallow, and other products of the region. But, most important for the boy William, the estate included a very large plantation of an exceptional number of varieties of trees, including extensive orchards of peaches and apples. Here the boy found many kinds of birds and other animals which he had not known before, and he learned to watch and love them. He also became increasingly acquainted with the human population, as people visited the store, often coming from long distances.

The period of Hudson's boyhood in Argentina was one of almost incredible violence and recurring warfare. The ascendancy of the dictator Rosas was marked by recurring insurrections bloodily put down and by a general carelessness of civil rights and of human life itself. Later in his youth Hudson served for two brief periods in the army as a conscript during the fatuous but sanguinary war with Paraguay. This part of his early experience contributed to his first book to be published, the romantic novel *The Purple Land* (first called *The Purple Land that England Lost*).

Hudson's father was a man of ability and courage; on one occasion he probably saved the lives of his wife and children by his self-possession when a group of renegade soldiers stopped at the *estancia* demanding horses; for the threatening visitors concluded from his manner that he had a formidable armed guard secreted in the house and galloped away. But Daniel Hudson was a poor businessman; he lost money steadily at "The Acacias"—while, at the same time, constantly spending it for improvements; he was far too generous in extending credit; and it developed finally that he had never secured a firm legal title to the property. The result was the family's return to the now reduced *estancia* of "The Twenty-five Ombú Trees," when William was sixteen.

In the preceding year, when William Hudson was fifteen, he suffered a very prolonged illness. Apparently he had contracted typhus fever while on a visit to Buenos Aires. Before he had fully recovered from the effects of this illness, a long day of exposure while driving some newly purchased and stubborn cattle brought on an attack of rheumatic fever, an extremely long and severe illness which threatened his life, enfeebled him for many months, and left him with a permanently damaged heart and uncertain health at best. The only beneficial result of these illnesses was the opportunity provided for much reading in the relatively large and well-chosen family library, which included many books about history. The gravity of the second illness brought fear of death, and that, with his reading, contributed to the rise of religious doubts. Shortly thereafter, when William had just turned eighteen, Hudson's mother died. The passages dealing with her character and her concern for her son's religious faith are among the most poignant in *Far Away and Long Ago*—indeed, in the whole literature of autobiography.

As Hudson's strength increased after the second severe illness, he resumed the previously established habit of solitary days on the pampas and along the watercourses, primarily devoted to observation of birds. After his father died in 1868, his home was the house of a friend in Buenos Aires. His occupation in his early manhood, until his move to England in 1874, remained a mystery until the publication of his *Letters On the Ornithology of Buenos Ayres* in 1951. These letters show that during this period he supported himself chiefly as a collector of bird skins for museums—first for the Natural History Museum of Buenos Aires, then for the Smithsonian Institution of Washington, D.C., and finally for the Zoological Society of London. Since the birds of Argentina were relatively unknown in the scientific world at that time, the specimens found a ready market. In his later years

Hudson strongly condemned the killing of birds for scientific
or other collections, and his reticence as to his first gainful occupation is, therefore, understandable.

His first published writings, which appeared in the *Proceedings* of the London Zoological Society in 1870 and 1871 in the
form of letters, were written at Hudson's suggestion in response
to encouragement from Dr. P. L. Sclater of the society. One of
these letters is notable because it contains a vigorous attack on
Darwin for what Hudson read as an erroneous account of the
habits of a certain Argentinian woodpecker: an attack dignified
by Darwin by a detailed but courteous rebuttal. In these early
years of his manhood Hudson's ambition clearly was to become
known and honored as a scientist, specifically as an ornithologist.
In furtherance of his objective and in fulfillment of a desire
first consciously felt in childhood, Hudson spent most of the
year 1871 in the remote southern region of Argentina known as
Patagonia. His experience there became the major substance of
Idle Days in Patagonia, a book not published until 1893. His
motivation for this expedition rose partly from his boyhood observation of birds migrating to and from Patagonia and partly
from his hope to discover new species—thus gaining scientific
fame—in that little-known region. He did collect and send to the
London Zoological Society one new species, and he was honored
by Dr. Sclater's naming the bird for him, *Cnipolegus hudsoni.*
It appears probable that the work which appeared in two
volumes as *Argentine Ornitholgy* in 1888-89, with the scientific
data supplied by Sclater and with the accounts of habits and
characteristics by Hudson, may have been contemplated by both
men before Hudson's departure from Argentina. In any case,
Hudson sailed for England in 1874, at the age of thirty-three,
never to return to Argentina or, indeed, to either America.

When he arrived in England, Hudson was welcomed and for
a time entertained by the family of a young Englishman who
had become his warm friend in Argentina. But he shortly had
to face the problem of earning a living, since he had neither
inherited money nor earned more as a collector than a subsistence income. It seems probable that work on the *Argentine
Ornithology* with Dr. Sclater was begun shortly, but it is certain
that payment for this work was small, if it was forthcoming at
all. Under the stimulus of his discovery of pleasure in writing

and the encouragement of the publication of his letters to Dr. Sclater, Hudson attempted to make a living by writing. Only a few samples of the writing he undertook during the next ten years have either survived or been identified. Not until eleven years after his arrival was his first novel published, *The Purple Land* (1885); but it failed to earn much money.

Not long after Hudson embarked on a literary career in London, he married in 1877 Emily Wingrave, a woman who was according to some accounts fifteen, in others twenty, years his senior—which means that she was about fifty. At the time of their marriage Emily Wingrave was operating a boardinghouse—presumably inexpensive; it is reasonable to suppose that Hudson was a boarder and that the relationship grew from her kindness to him. In any event, the boardinghouse failed, possibly because of Emily's sharing with Hudson's father a too great freedom in extending credit. There were other boardinghouses, which also failed. Emily tried to augment the slender and undependable income from her husband's writing by giving music lessons: in earlier years she had been a concert singer of some small reputation.

Although some students of Hudson, including Haymaker, consider that "the marriage was a blunder,"[1] they have failed to recognize the significance of the fact that there is no indication whatever that Emily tried to persuade her husband to turn to some occupation which would provide a stable income. On the contrary, there is abundant evidence that she shared his interest in birds in particular and in the earth in general. Whenever a manuscript sale provided a few pounds above immediate necessities, the two made excursions together into the British countryside, and these continued as long as Mrs. Hudson's health permitted. Hudson's letters, both to Morley Roberts and to Edward Garnett, contain references to these expeditions, to the couple's attending concerts and visiting art galleries together, and in very many instances to their reading of the same newly published or older books. Whenever they were separated for a day or longer—which occurred increasingly in periods of illness which both underwent in their later years together—Hudson wrote to his wife every day. The whole body of evidence seems, therefore, to demonstrate not only mutual devotion but a mutually helpful and appreciated relationship.

In spite of the appearance of some of Hudson's best writing in the decades following the marriage, their poverty continued and was often acute. For one week they had no food but a can of cocoa and a box of crackers. During these years of poverty, from the time of his arrival in England in 1874 almost to the end of the century, Hudson became only too well acquainted with the seamy side of London life, with the problems of extreme poverty, and with agitations for reform. Though he himself took no active part in reform movements, he portrayed the conditions and their consequences vividly in the pseudonymous novel *Fan* (1892). He did, however, become a propagandist in behalf of preservation of birds.

The period was one of extravagant use of the feathers of both native and exotic birds in feminine apparel; it was also a period in which the collection of mounted specimens of rare and beautiful birds, for display in drawing rooms and other private collections, was popular. Against both of these current fashions Hudson became a vigorous and effective protester. He was instrumental in the formation of the Society for the Protection of Birds (later the Royal Society for the Protection of Birds), and he wrote in its support a number of pamphlets, some of which have not yet been reprinted. Partly as a result of these activities, Hudson was granted in 1901 an annual civil-list pension of 150 pounds, largely through the efforts of Lord Grey, who admired Hudson's writing. Somewhat earlier Emily had inherited an old house which, though heavily mortgaged, provided a more permanent abode than they had had before; and it also enabled them to rely in part for support on rented portions of it. It was not until World War I that the success of a new American publisher, Alfred A. Knopf, in winning enormous sales in the United States for Hudson's *Green Mansions* (first published in England in 1904) meant that the Hudsons' financial problems were finally ended. Characteristically, Hudson promptly relinquished the pension.

During the last thirty years of his life, indeed from 1880 on, Hudson was more or less involved in the contemporary literary scene in London; for, through the friendship of two much younger men, Morley Roberts and Edward Garnett, he became acquainted with it. Hudson's surviving letters to these friends, collected and published after his death, provide our best insights into Hudson's later years and, as we shall see in Chapter 8, also give information about Hudson's literary indebtednesses and enthusiasms.

The health of both Hudson and his wife, always uncertain, grew more so as they aged. Indeed, Emily was a confirmed invalid for the last ten years of her life; in the last few years before her death in 1921, she was bedridden and was constantly cared for by a nurse. During this same period, Hudson himself underwent recurring periods of prolonged and severe illness. In one of these and during his slow recovery in a convent hospital in Cornwall, in 1915-16, he began writing the autobiographical book about his boyhood on the pampas, *Far Away and Long Ago* (1918). After the completion of this book, he produced some of the essays collected in his remaining volumes; and he also prepared for the press his monumental study of the birds he had observed as a boy and young man; this work appeared in two large volumes as *Birds of La Plata* (1920). It contains Hudson's contributions to the *Argentine Anthology* (1888-89) by P. L. Sclater and Hudson, which had appeared in a very small edition. A major purpose in this work and his other latest books was to augment his bequest to the Society for the Protection of Birds, to which he left his estate. Meanwhile, the weakness of the heart which had its source in the rheumatic fever, following overexposure when he was a boy on the pampas, grew worse and more threatening; and it eventually caused his death, on August 18, 1922.

CHAPTER 2

Autobiographical Writings

IN a very real sense, nearly all of the writing of W. H. Hudson
may be viewed as essentially autobiographical—all, indeed,
except the fiction. What we find in Hudson's works, characteristically and constantly, is a rich and powerful sharing of actual
experience between writer and reader. This quality is apparent
even in the writings primarily scientific in purpose, as in *Birds
of La Plata* and *British Birds*. We are in a specific and clearly
felt and visioned place at a specific season and hour; there we
see and hear birds, plants, insects, other animals—and often men.
Through the magic of Hudson's style, his experience becomes
ours with the precision, the clarity, the vitality so often lacking
even in our apprehension of what we call "real" experience.

I Far Away and Long Ago

Only one of Hudson's books, however, is wholly and avowedly
autobiographical in the usual sense: *Far Away and Long Ago*.
The first draft of this book was written, as we have noted, in
Cornwall in the winter of 1916, while Hudson was in a nursing
home attached to a Roman Catholic convent, recovering from a
severe illness. He tells us in the first chapter how the book came
into being:

On the second day of my illness, during an interval of comparative
ease, I fell into recollection of my childhood, and at once I had that
far, that forgotten past with me again as I had never previously had it.
. . . What a happiness it would be, I thought, in spite of discomfort and
pain, if this vision would continue! It was not to be expected: never-
theless it did not vanish. . . . Propped up with pillows I began with
pencil and writing-pad to put it down in some sort of order, and went
on with it during the whole six weeks of my confinement, and in this
way produced the first rough draft of the book.[1]

The home of Hudson's very earliest memories—before he was five—was at "The Twenty-five Ombú Trees." Since the name is a strange one and occurs also in the title of one of Hudson's greatest works of fiction, the long story "El Ombú," it is worthwhile to quote part of his description of these trees:

. . . gigantic in size, and standing wide apart in a row about four hundred yards long. The ombú is a very singular tree indeed, and being the only representative of tree-vegetation, natural to the soil, on those great level plains, and having also many curious superstitions connected with it, it is a romance in itself. It belongs to the rare Phytolacca family, and has an immense girth—forty or fifty feet in some cases; at the same time the wood is so soft and spongy that it can be cut with a knife, and is utterly unfit for firewood, for when cut up it refuses to dry, but simply rots away like a ripe water-melon. It also grows slowly, and its leaves, which are large, glossy, and deep green, like laurel leaves, are poisonous.[2]

These earliest memories in the first chapter include the house, very old and rambling and supposed to be haunted; a crippled stray dog which became the children's pet; the herd of four or five hundred wild cattle being driven in at night by the herdsmen; and a picture of his mother watching the children at play. He also vividly pictures a neighbor, Captain Scott, an Englishman, who always brought the children sugarplums, and another less frequent visitor, a beggar, garmented most fantastically, who made his petition in "a strange language, which might have been Hebrew or Sanscrit, for there was no person learned enough in the country to understand it."[3]

When William was five, the family moved to the combined home and commercial establishment, with the great fruit orchard and park of other trees mentioned in the biographical chapter, "The Acacias." From this point the memories, which broaden and deepen in accordance with the boy's years, assume the range and power which fully justify the judgment that this book is one of the finest of autobiographies. There are people—the portrayals ranging from the vivid glimpse of the apprehended murderer tied in the great barn awaiting the arrival of the police ("a man, sitting or crouching on the floor, his hands before him, the wrists tied together, his body bound with thongs of raw hide to a big post"),[4] whom the Hudson children encounter in their first exploration of their new home—to the richly detailed, leisurely, and sustained accounts of neighbors and frequent visitors.

Among the vivid, interesting characters they meet, we find Barboza, of the "immense crow-black beard," a famous gaucho fighter (at least by reputation) and a singer of ballads. Mr. Royd, an English sheep farmer with a native wife, serves memorable dinners; Don Gandara, who "had a round or barrel-shaped body, short bow legs, and a big round head, which resembled a ball fashioned out of a block of dark-coloured wood with a coarse human face and huge ears rudely carved on it,"[5] has a passion for piebald horses; he kept about a thousand brood mares, nearly all piebalds. He was also the possessor of—or possessed by—a pet ostrich, which afforded abundant amusement to the Hudson children on their visits to his establishment.

Perhaps the finest portrait is that of Don Evaristo, whom Hudson calls "A Patriarch of the Pampas": he had six wives, all living with him in the same house, and numerous children. Hudson tells us that this man was esteemed and loved above most of the landowners because of his kindness to poor people and his willingness to serve them. The public attitude was: "If it pleased such a man to have six wives instead of one it was right and proper for him to have them; no person would presume to say that he was not a good and wise and religious man on that account."[6]

Among the other most vivid and fully realized of the many sketches of people outside the family in *Far Away and Long Ago* are the portrayals of the three tutors who, one after another and each for a brief period, provided W. H. Hudson with all the formal education he ever received, except for the instruction given him by his mother. The first, a Mr. Trigg, was a competent teacher but "a sort of Jekyll and Hyde, all pleasantness in one of his states and all black looks and truculence in the other." He "was finally got rid of because in one of his demoniacal moods he thrashed us brutally with his horsewhip."[7] A second tutor for a brief period was a Roman Catholic priest, who was milder and much less efficient; and the third, a brilliant young Englishman, earned the admiration of Hudson's oldest brother for his knowledge of mathematics, and he succeeded "in rousing a certain enthusiasm" in his other charges. Unfortunately, he was a victim of alcoholism and soon departed.

Hudson's portrayal of his mother permeates the book, through brief repeated glimpses: we see her acts of kindness to neighbors, by which she gained their respect and love even though she was, in the eyes of these emotional Roman Catholics, a heretic and a lost soul; her courage and resourcefulness, her concern for her children, and her affection for each, widely differing as they were. Hudson's relationship with her was a close one:

In my individual case there was more, a secret bond of union between us, since she best understood my feeling for Nature and sense of beauty, and recognized that in this I was nearest to her. Thus, besides and above the love of mother and son, we had a spiritual kinship, and this was so much to me that everything beautiful in sight or sound that affected me came associated with her to my mind. . . . All things beautiful, but chiefly flowers. Her feeling for them was little short of adoration.[8]

His mother's favorite flowers, Hudson tells us, were not the roses and carnations in our gardens,

"but the wild flowers growing on the pampas—flowers which I never see in England. I remember them, and if by some strange chance I should find myself once more in that distant region, I should go out in search of them, and seeing them again, feel that I was communing with her spirit."[9]

Actually, portrayals of people and experiences with them afford the larger part of *Far Away and Long Ago*. There are, however, interwoven with these, glimpses of the impressions made on the sensitive boy by places and by specific encounters with living nonhuman things. The sense of the vast plain of the pampas is felt recurringly, though only once does Hudson ask the reader to view it with him imaginatively:

We see all round us a flat land, its horizon a perfect ring of misty blue colour where the crystal-blue dome of the sky rests on the level green world. Green in late autumn, winter, and spring, or say from April to November, but not at all like a green lawn or field: there were smooth areas where sheep had pastured but the surface varied greatly and was mostly more or less rough. In places the land as far as one could see was covered with a dense growth of cardoon thistles, or wild artichoke, of a bluish or grey-green colour, while in other places the giant thistle flourished, a plant with big variegated green and white leaves, and standing when in flower six to ten feet high.[10]

One of the most noteworthy of Hudson's descriptive passages in this book is his impression of the blossoming peach trees at "The Acacias":

In August the peach blossomed. The great old trees standing wide apart on their grassy carpet, barely touching each other with the tips of their widest branches, were like great mound-shaped clouds of exquisite rosy-pink blossoms. . . . Even now when I recall the sight of those old flowering peach trees, with trunks as thick as a man's body, and the huge mounds of clouds of myriads of roseate blossoms seen against the blue ethereal sky, I am not sure that I have seen anything in my life more perfectly beautiful. Yet this great beauty was but half the charm I found in these trees: the other half was in the bird-music that issued from them.[11]

There is, as we might expect, much about birds in *Far Away and Long Ago;* however, this subject, so characteristic of Hudson, is subordinated, like the descriptions of places, to the portrayals of people. One of his most vivid accounts concerns his first sight of flamingos, where he had been taken by one of his older brothers on a long walk across the plain to a river some two miles away:

An astonishing number of birds were visible . . . but the most wonderful of all were three immensely tall white-and-rose coloured birds, wading solemnly in a row a yard or so apart from one another some twenty yards out from the bank. I was amazed and enchanted at the sight, and my delight was intensified when the leading bird stood still, and, raising his head and long neck aloft, opened and shook his wings. For the wings when open were of a glorious crimson color, and the bird to me was the most angel-like creature on earth.[12]

The seventeenth chapter of *Far Away and Long Ago,* "A Boy's Animism," is central in the understanding of the book as a whole because of its candid illumination of Hudson's most profound experiences and attitudes. He begins with a definition:

"by animism I do not mean the theory of a soul in nature, but the tendency or impulse or instinct, in which all myth originates, to *animate* all things; the projection of ourselves into nature; the sense and apprehension of an intelligence like our own but more powerful in all visible things."[13]

Hudson expresses his belief that this feeling "persists and lives in many of us, I imagine, more than we like to think, or more than we know";[14] but he also admits that "In large towns and all populous places, where nature has been tamed until it looks like a part of man's work, almost as artificial as the buildings he inhabits, it withers and dies so early in life that its faint intimations are soon forgotten and we come to believe that we have never experienced them."[15]

The feeling of the supernatural in nature, the animism which he was discussing, Hudson tells us, "was evoked more powerfully by trees than by even the most supernatural of my flowers; it varied in power according to time and place and the appearance of the tree or trees, and always affected me most on moonlight nights." When he crept out of the house at night and stood "silent and motionless, near some group of large trees," his sense of some mystery in them grew so strong that he became frightened and fled to the lighted rooms of his home. "Yet on the very next night I would steal out again and go to the spot where the effect was strongest, which was usually among the large locust or white acacia trees, which gave the name of Las Acacias to our place. The loose feathery foliage on moonlight nights had a peculiar hoary aspect that made this tree seem more intensely alive than others, more conscious of my presence and watchful of me."[16]

Although Hudson received religious instruction by his devout mother, he was less impressed with what he learned than he was by what he experienced:

But apart from the fact that the powers above would save me in the end from extinction, which was a great consolation, these teachings did not touch my heart as it was touched and thrilled by something nearer, more intimate, in nature, not only in moonlit trees or in a flower or serpent, but, in certain exquisite moments and moods and in certain aspects of nature, in "every grass" and in all things, animate and inanimate.[17]

This remarkable chapter about animism closes with examples of conscious tree worship on the part of some deeply religious and highly intellectual persons and of a few primitive people in rural England.

The final chapters of Hudson's account of his boyhood—"Boyhood's End," "A Darkened Life," and "Loss and Gain"—recount his experience of the two severe illnesses in his teen-age years. In these years his religious beliefs, gained from his mother, crumbled because of the effects of the wide reading he undertook following the first illness, but chiefly because of the impact of the decision of the doctors that he would not recover from the second illness and was destined to an early death. Hudson did not confess his doubts to his mother; but "she knew it all, and I knew that she knew."[18] Her death, which occurred during these years of the boy's great mental and spiritual suffering, intensified his distress. Only when Hudson began slowly but unmistakably to recover from his second illness did he begin to believe that a life filled with interest and usefulness might still be his. His earlier religious faith was gone, never to be regained; but he found increasing reason to rejoice in living.

Among the most important events of the years covered in these final chapters are two reading experiences (both to be discussed later in this study). One of these was Gilbert White's *Selborne,* "given to me by an old friend of our family," who had bought it for him on a trip to London, thinking "that it was just the right thing to get for that bird-loving boy out on the pampas."[19] The other profoundly important reading experience of these years was Darwin's *The Origin of Species,* loaned to him by his older brother, who had returned to Argentina after study abroad. When Hudson was questioned by his brother about his opinion of the book, William told him that "Darwin had only succeeded in disproving his own theory with his argument from natural selection;"[20] his brother only laughed and advised him to read the book again. William did, and he continued for years to argue the problem with himself. He tells us, on the last page but one of the autobiography: "Insensibly and inevitably I had become an evolutionist, albeit never wholly satisfied with natural selection as the only and sufficient explanation of the change in the forms of life. And again, insensibly and inevitably, the new doctrine had led to modifications of the old religious ideas and eventually to a new and simplified philosophy of life."[21]

The return of Hudson's health and the gradual realization that he could reasonably hope for and "count on thirty, forty, even fifty years with their summers and autumns and winters" renewed and redirected the forces of his mind and soul; but the results of his possible death had lingering results: "When I hear people say that they have not found the world and life so agreeable or interesting as to be in love with it, or that they look with equanimity to its end, I am apt to think they have never been properly alive nor seen with clear vision the world they think so meanly of, or anything in it—not a blade of grass."[22] Hudson confesses that he realizes his is "an exceptional case, that the visible world is to me more beautiful and interesting than to most persons," but he affirms that his happiness in nature and the earth was never lost, "so that in my worst times, when I was compelled to exist shut out from Nature in London for long periods, sick and poor and friendless, I could yet always feel that it was infinitely better to be than not to be."[23]

II Idle Days in Patagonia

Though most of the essays which make up *Idle Days in Patagonia* (1892) are scientific in emphasis the relatively few autobiographical chapters are of such crucial importance in their revelation of the initiation and direction of Hudson's whole later career that this volume requires consideration in the autobiographical group. The first one hundred pages which are essentially autobiographical are devoted to brilliant narration of adventurous experience. In 1871, Hudson, encouraged by the recognition he was receiving from the London Zoological Society and in fulfillment of a long-sustained wish to follow migrants southward in the Argentinian autumn, set out for Patagonia. He made the trip south in an old coastal steamer, which went aground not far from the mouth of the Río Negro. Hudson and three companions left the vessel and set out for the river and the town of El Carmen. They had not anticipated the hardships they encountered in crossing miles of desert on foot. Close to exhaustion and suffering from thirst, they at last reached the river. Hudson spent twelve months in its valley and the adjacent desert, but the area was not precisely what he had expected. He did make a valuable collection of the birds of the region, though he found only one new species—he had hoped to discover six or seven. When he sent this newly found bird with the rest of his collection to the London Zoological Society, the previously unknown species—a black tyrant bird—was promptly named *Cnipolegus hudsoni* in his honor.

But shortly after Hudson's arrival in Patagonia he was crippled; accidentally shot in the knee from a revolver with the hand of a friend. Months of enforced idleness ensued while the injury slowly healed, and this was followed by more months of voluntary idleness: it was a period in which Hudson rode without purpose day after day in the desert, engaged in a half-conscious process of self-discovery and redirection. The young man who was eager to achieve distinction as a scientist—possibly to be a rival of Darwin—perished in these months; from him emerged the seer, the worshiper of earth, the possessor of knowledge and understanding greater than those of any seeker for strictly limited scientific knowledge—the Hudson we find in his greatest books.

The autobiographical chapters of *Idle Days in Patagonia* are marked by the brilliant renderings of people, places, animals, and plants that we also find in *Far Away and Long Ago:* a gambler friend, a white man turned Indian, a hunting dog, the desert itself. But the deeper significance of Hudson's Patagonian experience almost escapes even his great powers of expression. It emerges by glimpses in the chapter "The War with Nature" and by constant implication in the chapter "Idle Days." During his isolation in Patagonia Hudson found himself and the main direction of his life: the attainment of understanding beyond knowledge and the communication of it to others. In Chapter 8 of *Idle Days in Patagonia*, "Snow, and the Quality of Whiteness," the book suddenly changes direction and emphasis. It is especially interesting as the sole example in Hudson's early work of what may be regarded as extended literary criticism; it is notably so to the student of American literature because it is devoted to a study of the famous Chapter 42 of Melville's *Moby Dick*, "The Whiteness of the Whale." It is probable that Melville was more widely known and read in England at the time of his death in 1892 than he was in America. In any case, it is clear that Hudson had read *Moby Dick* thoughtfully and that this chapter had impressed and especially interested him. He refers to it as "a long dissertation, perhaps the finest thing in the book";[24] and he speaks later of "that feeling, so powerfully described by Melville, at the sight of the muffled rollings of a milky sea."

Hudson comments that in Melville this feeling "was very

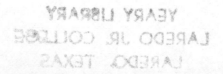

strong; it stirred him deeply, and caused him to ponder with awe on its meaning; and the conclusion he came to was that it is an instinct in us. . . . He calls it an inherited experience." Developing his interpretation of Melville's view and using diction and rhythms strongly suggestive of those most characteristic of Melville, Hudson continues: "the feeling speaks to us of appalling things in a remote past, of unimaginable desolations, and stupendous calamities overwhelming the race of man."[25]

Hudson continues his appreciative comment, in a paragraph stylistically worthy of its subject:

It is a sublime conception, adequately expressed; and as we read the imagination pictures to us the terrible struggle of our hardy barbarous progenitors against the bitter killing cold of the last glacial period; but the picture is vague, like striving human figures in a landscape half obliterated by wind-driven snow. It was a struggle that endured for long ages, until the gigantic white phantom, from which men sought everywhere to fly, came to be a phantom of the mind, a spectralness over the fancy, and instinctive horror, which the surviving remnant transmitted by inheritance down to our own distant times.[26]

Although Hudson gives a fair statement of Melville's theory and generous recognition to his expression of it, he does not agree with it. Fear of snow, and of whiteness in general, is not, Hudson prefers to think, instinctive:

That mysterious something that moves us at the sight of snow springs from the animism that exists in us, and our animistic way of regarding all exceptional phenomena. The mysterious feelings produced in us by the sight of a snow-whitened earth are not singular, but are similar in character to the feelings caused by many other phenomena, and they may be experienced, although in a very slight degree, almost any day of our lives, if we live with nature.[27]

When Hudson proceeds again to explain what he means by "animism," he carefully differentiates his meaning from that of the term as used by cultural anthropologists: "Animism . . . means not a doctrine of souls that survive the bodies and objects they inhabit, but the mind's projection of itself into nature, its attribution of its own sentient life and intelligence to all things. . . ." He then adds a characteristic comment:

When our philosophers tell us that this faculty is obsolete in us, that it is effectually killed by ratiocination, or that it only survives for a period in our children, I believe they are wrong, a fact which they could find out for themselves if, leaving their books and theories, they would take a solitary walk on a moonlit night in the "Woods of Westermain," or any other woods, since all are enchanted.[28]

The remaining essays in *Idle Days in Patagonia,* widely varied in subject matter, include a long discussion of "Bird Music in South America," two slightly related essays on "Sight in Savages" and "Concerning Eyes," an essay totally unrelated to the other contents of the book on "The Perfume of an Evening Primrose," and two in which the autobiographical aspect of the volume reappears in some degree: "Idle Days" and "The Plains of Patagonia." The essay on bird music professes in its title to include the whole of South America in its scope; and, for the portions of the continent which Hudson did not know from personal experience, he quotes the same authorities he had consulted in writing *Green Mansions,* notably *The Naturalist on the River Amazons,* by H. W. Bates, and *Among the Indians of Guiana,* by Everard im Thurn.

In the essay "Sight in Savages" Hudson argues that uncivilized men do not actually have better vision than their civilized fellows; they have simply learned from long and often painful experience to see what it is important for them to observe. The essay "Concerning Eyes," chiefly devoted to the color of them, includes a narrative of Hudson's search in London, on streets and omnibuses, for eyes actually and genuinely green: the search failed. This essay includes a reference to Hawthorne. Hudson quotes from the recently published biography of Hawthorne his wife's vivid and memorable description of Hawthorne's eyes: "I never dared gaze at him, even I, unless his lids were down." Hudson comments: "I think we have, most of us, seen eyes like these—eyes which one rather avoids meeting, because when met one is startled by the sight of a naked human soul brought so near."[29]

There are references in the essays to John Burroughs, whose writings in general Hudson liked and whose *Impressions of Some British Song Birds* he calls "excellent" in the essay on bird music. Several references are to Thoreau, who was the American writer most important to Hudson and most frequently cited by him. Most of these occur in the essay, "The Plains of Patagonia." Commenting on the pleasure found by children (and adults) in discovering wild food, and the American fashion of eating with delight, when we ourselves discover it in the wilderness, food which we would normally reject, Hudson quotes Thoreau: "As I came through the wood, I caught a glimpse of a woodchuck stealing across my path, and felt a strange thrill of savage delight, and was strongly tempted to seize and devour him raw; not that I was hungry then, except for the wildness which he represented."[30] A few pages later he cites Thoreau's response to the evening song of a robin. Five pages later Hudson describes himself as one of those who "have their instincts nearer to the surface, and are moved deeply by nature in any solitary place," and he adds: "I imagine that Thoreau was such a one."[31]

This essay, "The Plains of Patagonia," and "Idle Days" earlier in the volume, especially the latter, contain the crux of Hudson's experience in Patagonia; but they show that he seemingly did not fully understand what was happening to him. Inexplicably, he found his eager purpose to extend his collections and to gain scientific fame by discovery of new species fading, losing its power. In "Idle Days" he tells how, day after day and week after week, he aimlessly rode on the desert plains or rested in the rare shade: he was doing nothing purposeful, not even thinking; he was simply existing. In the essay later in the volume, "The Plains of Patagonia," he pictures the place as one that "has a look of antiquity, of desolation, of eternal peace, of a desert that has been a desert from of old and will continue a desert forever. . . ."[32] These remarkable essays succeed, as Hudson's writings characteristically do, because of the concrete vicarious experience they give us so richly. We ride aimlessly with Hudson; we find a chance spot of shade and lie down to rest; we fill our eyes hour after hour with the always repeated spacious vision of desolation; and, with him, we come gradually to a renewed realization of personal being and of the integrity of the deepest personal purpose. To clinch the importance of the process of self-discovery which these essays reveal, Hudson returns to Melville, citing what he calls "one of the most eloquent passages of his finest work," and quoting in full the famous passage in Chapter 26 of *Moby Dick* beginning; "Men may seem detestable as joint-stock companies and nations. . . ." On the facing page, in the final brief paragraph of the essay, he notes: "Thoreau, albeit so spiritually minded, could yet 'reverence' that lower nature in him which made him brother to the brute. He experienced and fully appreciated its tonic effect."[33]

On "The Plains of Patagonia" Hudson experienced a gradual and profound redirection, both practical and spiritual. The simple animism of his childhood was recovered in new and deeper meaning. The ambitous young scientist perished, to be replaced by the lover of all life, the seer and persuasive prophet of a new relation to nature, the worshiper of earth.

CHAPTER 3

The Naturalist

THE *Naturalist in La Plata* (1892) is a very important book in its relation to Hudson's whole literary career. In the first place, it achieved a moderate degree of financial and critical success, in contrast to the total failure of the early novels, *The Purple Land* and *A Crystal Age,* and *Fan,* published in the same year. Two printings of *The Naturalist in La Plata* were called for within the year of publication and a third only three years later, Furthermore, it was widely and favorably reviewed. For the first time, Hudson could therefore feel that his literary ambitions had at least a degree of justification.

I *Insects and Birds*

The Naturalist in La Plata differs widely in significant ways from the subsequent books of essays. In the first place, it lacks the unity of material and purpose which marks most of the later volumes. Its wide range of subject matter may be suggested by a half-dozen of the twenty-four chapter titles: "Some Curious Animal Weapons," "Fear in Birds," "A Noble Wasp," "Music and Dancing in Nature," "The Woodhewer Family," "The Strange Instincts of Cattle," "Facts and Thoughts About Spiders." Only four of the twenty-four essays are devoted to birds, in contrast to the general emphasis seen in most of Hudson's later volumes. Seven are on insects, an emphasis not repeated in any later Hudson volume. Most of the material of observation utilized throughout the book is drawn from Hudson's Argentinian experience; he had not yet begun to depend primarily on the fruits of his travels in England.

A second major difference between *The Naturalist in La Plata* and the later collections of essays lies in its emphasis on matters of scientific theory rather than on observation and experience

for their own sake. Again and again in the essays of this first
volume the direction and substance are determined by some
general scientific conception which Hudson is supporting, suggesting, or in many cases attacking. Most prominent are Hudson's
attacks on Darwin's theories of natural and sexual selection.
Repeatedly he presents facts, of his own observation most frequently, which conflict with Darwin's views or tend to throw
doubts on them. The general concept of evolution he has fully
accepted: "we are familiar with the truth that in organic nature
great things result from small beginnings—a common flower,
and our own bony skulls, to say nothing of the matter contained
within them, are proofs of it."[1] But this observation occurs in
the chapter "Music and Dancing in Nature," in which Hudson
most vigorously attacks Darwin about the theory of sexual selection as accounting for the songs of birds and the play of animals
in general. Hudson holds that birds sing simply because they enjoy singing—not just as a means of attracting a mate—and that
their forms of play, of which he gives some remarkable and most
interesting examples, are individually and socially motivated and
have little or nothing to do with mating.

Hudson points out, to support his view, that "In some migrants
the males arrive before the females, and no sooner have they
recovered from the effects of their journey than they burst out
into rapturous singing; these are not love-strains, since the females have not arrived, and pairing-time is perhaps a month
distant; their singing merely expresses their overflowing gladness." He adds the observation that "some birds that are good
melodists at other times sing in a feeble, disjointed manner during
courtship."[2] He concludes his argument, in this long chapter,
with this firm statement of his disagreement with Darwin:

I am convinced that any student of the subject who will cast aside his
books—supposing that they have not already bred a habit in his mind
of seeing only "in accordance with verbal statement"—and go directly
to nature to note the actions of animals for himself—actions which, in
many cases, appear to lose all significance when set down in writing—
the result of such independent investigation will be a conviction that
conscious sexual selection on the part of the female is not the cause of
music and dancing performances in birds, nor of the brighter colours
and ornaments that distinguish the male.[3]

In support of his objection Hudson had previously marshaled a large number of examples—especially of the strange customs of birds—drawn from his observations recorded in the *Argentine Ornithology*.

No doubt the exotic material contained in the volume contributed to the interest of contemporary readers; the readiness to disagree with Darwin and the ability to marshal evidence for his disagreement surely did, since the "Darwinian controversy" was still very much alive. Herbert Spencer is quoted, and the names of other scientists, especially of entomologists (in accordance with the relatively large space devoted to consideration of insects in this book) appear more frequently in *The Naturalist in La Plata* than in the subsequent volumes of essays. Included also rather frequently are the observations of other scientists in South America. Specifically cited are Thomas Belt's *The Naturalist in Nicaragua* (later noted in connection with *A Crystal Age*); H. W. Bates' *The Naturalist on the River Amazons*, and Everard F. im Thurn's *Among the Indians of Guiana*, noted in connection with *Green Mansions*.

That Hudson's ambition for recognition as a scientific observer was not yet dead at the time of the appearance of this book—or at least when he was writing the individual essay—is suggested by his claim of first publication for the curious phenomenon described in the shortest essay of the volume, "Dragon-Fly Storms": the occasional flights of enormous numbers—millions—of dragonflies preceding a violent storm and change in temperature:

It is clear that these great and frequent dragon-fly movements are not explicable on any current hypothesis regarding the annual migration of butterflies, or the migrations of some mammals . . . "from a sense of polarity." Neither this hypothetical sense in animals, nor "historical memory" will account for the dragon-fly storms . . . since the insects do not pass and repass between "breeding and subsistence areas," but all journey in a north-easterly direction; and of the countless millions flying like thistle-down before the great pampero wind, not one solitary traveller ever returns.[4]

Though, as we have seen, *The Naturalist in La Plata* differs from the later and more characteristic volumes of Hudson's essays in lack of unity of subject matter and in other ways—

notably the emphasis on scientific controversy—it has much of his characteristic content and method. At the outset, Hudson identifies the Argentinian pampas as "my 'parish of Selborne' "— at least so far as this book is concerned—and only a few pages later, in the initial essay on "The Desert Pampas," Hudson characteristically admits his inability to share completely with the reader the experience he tries to present: "For the flight of the sea-mew is not more impossible to us than the power to picture forth the image of Nature in our souls, when she reveals herself in one of those 'special moments' which have 'special grace' in situations where her wild beauty has never been spoiled by man."[5]

In the same chapter, Hudson bewails the changes going on so rapidly on the pampas, among them the disappearance of the rhea, the South American ostrich: "the cowardly murderous methods of science, and a systematic war of extermination, have left him no chance. And with the rhea go the flamingo, antique and splendid; and the swans in their bridal plumage; and the rufous tinamou—sweet and mournful melodist of the eventide; and the noble crested screamer, that clarion-voiced watch-bird of the night wilderness."[6] Both the maturity and vigor of Hudson's characteristic style and its expression of his general attitudes in this and other passages make me feel that probably this first essay of the book was the latest in composition.

In this essay also Hudson expresses strongly an attitude which he admits may make him unpopular:

the forms of life in the two higher vertebrate classes are nature's most perfect work; and the life of even a single species is of incalculably greater value to mankind, for what it teaches and would continue to teach, than all the chiseled marbles and painted canvases the world contains; though doubtless there are many persons who are devoted to art, but blind to some things greater than art, who will set me down as a Philistine for saying so. And, above all others, we should protect and hold sacred those types, Nature's masterpieces, which are first singled out for destruction on account of their size, or splendour, or rarity, and that false detestable glory which is accorded to their most successful slayers.[7]

Then, with an eloquence rare in even his latest books, Hudson asserts the need for the careful preservation, rather than the purposeful destruction, of the rare and beautiful higher forms of life: "Like immortal flowers they have drifted down to us on the ocean of time, and their strangeness and beauty bring to our imaginations a dream and a picture of that unknown world, immeasurably far removed, where man was not: and when they perish, something of gladness goes out from nature, and the sunshine loses something of its brightness."[8] By the time of the publication of *The Naturalist in La Plata* in 1892, Hudson was well launched on his campaign for the protection of rare and vanishing British birds; and the attitude so vigorously expressed here is identical in tone and temper with that found in his polemical writings in that campaign.

It is not hard to see why *The Naturalist in La Plata* became a moderately popular book and still less so to understand why it produced a highly favorable response in discriminating readers. It introduced to most British readers of the 1890's what was essentially a new world—Argentina—in terms of some of its most interesting and individual forms of life. It dealt candidly with contemporary scientific problems, and it dared to challenge Darwin. It holds much of the richness of Hudson's concern and love for all living things which mark the whole body of his work. Its wide range of subjects, its occassional dry humor and frequent stylistic force and beauty, make it a good book for the beginning reader of Hudson today, just as it was for almost all of its readers in 1892.

II *The Scientific Studies of Birds*

The writings of W. H. Hudson which are essentially scientific in purpose and content form only a small part of his total production, and they have been generally ignored by critics. The fact is, however, that these writings are frequently marked by the literary qualities which distinguish his work as a whole—by his characteristic vividness and vitality of style and by his supreme capacity to convey his observed experience so strongly and richly as to make it become also the experience of the reader. For this reason, the scientific writings richly repay attention; indeed, they demand it if the full measure of Hudson's achievement as a writer is to be recognized.

Hudson's first writings to gain publication are to be found in a series of letters which he sent to Dr. P. L. Sclater of the London Zoological Society in 1869 and 1870, which were subsequently published in the *Proceedings* of the society. Numerous mistakes in spelling and occasional examples of faulty syntax in the letters as Hudson wrote them (corrected in the published form) testify to Hudson's lack of formal training as a writer. But frequently these earliest writings demonstrate not only Hudson's capacity for close observation but also the range and resourcefulness of his ability to make the reader share his experience. An example is his account of the black-headed gull in the letter of June 20, 1870. He tells how, "in seasons when Grasshoppers abound very much, flocks of these birds also appear" and form "a front of several thousand feet with a breadth of but sixty or eighty." The birds are in constant motion, "skimming along the ground with half expanded wing"; and, as they go, they leave the earth "free from the pest."[9]

An even more interesting example of this early quality in Hudson's writing is found in his account of the flight of the glossy ibis, in his letter of June 20, 1870: "A body of these birds on the wing is a most interesting sight—now soaring high in the air, displaying the deep chestnut hue of their chests, now descending with a graceful curve towards the earth, as if to exhibit the beautiful metallic green of their upper plumage."[10]

In the years immediately following Hudson's arrival in England in 1874, he collaborated with P. L. Sclater in the production of a two-volume work, *Argentine Ornithology*, published in 1888-89 and now rare. To it, Dr. Sclater contributed the scientific descriptions and classifications, but Hudson supplied the accounts of the habits of the various species. For this work he unerringly selected and used the more vivid and effective passages from the earlier letters, using these with only minor, or no, alterations. Thirty years later Hudson prepared his material used in this work for publication as *Birds of La Plata* (1920) in two handsome volumes with colored illustrations. Although he made some changes in the text, again the more vivid and eloquent passages of the early letters appear, virtually unchanged. In *Birds of La Plata*, the "flocks" of gulls become "a white cloud" as they settle on the fields, and their wings are "expanded," not "half-expanded." The assertion that they leave the earth "free from the pest" is dropped.[11] In the account of the flight of the glossy ibis, "the beautiful metallic green of their upper plumage" becomes the slightly more precise "dark metallic green and purple reflections of their upper plumage."[12]

The clearest and most abundant evidence for my claim that *Birds of La Plata*, in which Hudson's text is virtually identical with that of the early *Argentine Ornithology*, deserves attention for its literary quality, is found in Hudson's numerous attempts to express in words the experience of hearing the songs of birds. This emphasis is found recurringly in his writings, from the *Letters on the Ornithology of Buenos Ayres* on, often with overt recognition of the difficulty of the attempt and with the acknowledgment of the fascination which it held for him. Brilliant examples of his achievement in this field are abundant in *Birds of La Plata*. For every one of the some two hundred species discussed, Hudson makes some attempt to describe the bird's utterance; among the passages devoted to this purpose are examples of extremely vivid and impressive writing as Hudson attempts to enable the reader to hear the bird imaginatively.

Hudson's descriptions of the calls and songs of birds are not sentimental in any sense of conveying a falseness or a lack of reality. Of the blue tanager he writes: "The male emits a series of squealing sounds by way of song";[13] of the blue-and-yellow tanager, "the male has a song composed of a succession of sounds like the bleating of a kid."[14] The red-billed ground finches "have a loud, sharp alarm chirp or cry, which bursts from the bird with the startling suddenness of a sneeze from a human being; also a confused, unmelodious song, which always reminds me, in its hurry, vehemence, and peculiar sound, of the gobbling of a turkey-cock."[15]

These frank and uncomplimentary comments serve to reinforce and intensify the reader's appreciation of Hudson's rendering of the songs he admires, as in this comment: "where the Chingolos are very abundant the whole air, on a bright summer morning, is alive with their delicate melody; only one must pause and listen before one is aware of it, otherwise it will escape notice, owing to its thin ethereal character, the multitudinous notes not mingling but floating away, as it were, detached and scattered, mere gossamer webs of sound that very faintly impress the sense."[16]

CHAPTER 4

The Fiction

I The Purple Land

IN its most vital and interesting elements, Hudson's first novel
and his first independent publication, *The Purple Land*
(1885), is closely related to the autobiographical books of later
years discussed in Chapter 2: *Far Away and Long Ago* and *Idle
Days in Patagonia*. These elements are the dramatic presentations
of gaucho life on the pampas in the period of Hudson's own
earliest observation and the preceding years. Its structure is
episodic, and the individual dramatic incidents are held together
by a somewhat tenuous general framework.

The episodic structure of *The Purple Land* is indicated by
the fact that Hudson lifted one entire chapter from it, with only
a few minor textual changes, to appear as a short story in the
collection published as *El Ombú* in 1902: "The Story of a Piebald
Horse." In *The Purple Land,* this story is told by a gaucho and
listened to by the central character, Richard Lamb, in the course
of his adventures. The characterization of this central figure,
Richard Lamb, a young Englishman who has lived long in South
America, is fairly consistent. He is courageous, resourceful, highly
responsive to the attractiveness of women but ultimately faithful
to his wife. The young wife is wholly shadowy, but some of the
women with whom Lamb is involved in his adventures are brilliantly rendered and fully convincing. The most memorable
characterization of the book is that of Demetria: a woman
slightly older than Lamb, who offers him marriage and a vast
estate in order to escape from an intolerable situation. He does
rescue her, but he remains loyal to his wife.

For any reader, *The Purple Land* offers a highly individual,
colorful, and rewarding reading experience. To the student of
Hudson's writing as a whole, perhaps its most interesting passages

are those which link it with his later and more fully characteristic
writings. Prominent among these are references to birds and
especially to their voices. Lost in the dark, Lamb is startled
when "a large owl, flapping down close to my head, gave utterance to a long hiss, followed by a sharp clicking sound, ending
with a sudden loud, laughlike cry."[1] A hundred pages later,
when Lamb has survived both a battle and a fairly serious amor-
ous involvement and is escaping with some companions from a
battlefield, his observations are those of Hudson the naturalist:
"the querulous pipings of a flock of young black-headed siskins
flying about from tree to tree after their parents and asking to
be fed."[2]

After another hundred pages, Lamb—now separated from his
companions—spends a day alone in the forest; Hudson depicts
elements of this experience in a style and with a vividness comparable to those of his later work:

Presently I had some visitors in a flock of *urracas* . . . a graceful, loqua-
cious bird resembling a magpie, only with a longer tail and a bold,
red beak. These ill-mannered birds skulked about in the branches over
me all the time I remained in the wood, scolding me so incessantly in
their intolerably loud, angry, rattling notes, varied occasionally with
shrill whistlings and groans that I could scarcely even hear myself
think. They soon succeeded in bringing all the other birds within hear-
ing-distance to the spot to take part in their demonstration.[4]

Lamb's last visitor during this sojourn in the forest is reported
in the fresh, lively idiom which marks this first novel consistently:

an armadillo, that came hurrying towards me, looking curiously like a
little old bent-backed gentleman in a rusty black coat trotting briskly
about on some very important business. It came to within three yards of
my feet, then stopped, and seemed astonished beyond measure at my
presence, staring at me with its little, bleary, blinking eyes, and looking
more like the shabby old gentleman than ever. Then it trotted away
through the trees, but presently returned for a second inspection; and
after that it kept coming and going till I inadvertently burst out laugh-
ing, whereupon it scuttled away in great alarm, and returned no more.[5]

The signature of Hudson the naturalist, especially the ornithologist, is clearly written in these and other passages.

There are also in *A Purple Land* statements of Hudson's general attitudes, expressed in all his later work but usually in terms less overt and definite. Lamb reflects that "we are all vainly seeking after happiness in the wrong way." Bacon assured us that we had "only to conquer Nature" to be happy; "but how weary and sad we are getting! The old joy in life and gaiety of heart have vanished."[6]

Morley Roberts is justified in his observation that in *The Purple Land* Hudson "shines in character. Those he draws from the life stand upon their feet, or sit their horses, or squat upon a horse's head by a pampa fire and fight and talk and love like men."[7] Perhaps it was the vivid realism, the freedom from sentimentalism of the book—especially in the portrayal of all the feminine characters with the exception of the young wife—which repelled Victorian readers. In any case, *The Purple Land* is good reading today for any lover of fiction marked by vigorous action in an exotic setting; and attention is also justified as prelude and background for Hudson's later writing. However, the failure of *The Purple Land* to find readers or favorable reviewers—with a single exception[8]—on its publication in 1885 affords an interesting field for speculation. Hudson himself seemingly felt that the original title, *The Purple Land That England Lost*, was offensive to British pride, for he dropped the possibly invidious phrase "That England Lost" when the book was reissued.

II   A Crystal Age

A Crystal Age (1887), Hudson's second novel, is an anomaly in the whole body of his work; but it also expresses some of his most profound attitudes and beliefs. A dream-romance, the vision of a utopia, it relates the experience of one Smith—the name deliberately identifies him as a representative Englishman of Hudson's own time—who awakens from a mysterious sleep which is subsequently shown to have lasted thousands of years. Though Smith remembers only a fall while on a hunting expedition and finds himself still clothed in a woolen outdoor suit that has grown musty with time, no effort is made by Hudson to explain the circumstances in realistic terms.

As Smith wanders across a countryside recognizably English, yet strangely altered, he encounters a group of beautifully clothed and personally beautiful people who are engaged in a burial service. He is immediately seized by a profound admiration and passion for one of the number, seemingly a young girl, whose name is later revealed as Yoletta. He is keenly embarrassed by the contrast between his soiled and unlovely clothing and the beautiful attire of these strange people—and he immediate desires to be accepted by them. He is kindly accepted by the group, is fed and lodged, is promised new garments, and is given work to do to pay for them—the sovereigns he offers are rejected —in plowing a field with a primitive plow. Genuine humor appears in Hudson's treatment of this and other early experiences of Smith in the *Crystal Age:* when he displays his ignorance, the horses harness themselves to the plow; and they quit when they feel they have worked long enough.

Gradually, Smith learns something of the society into which he has come. Its center is the House: it is an extremely ancient and extremely beautiful structure, rich in the most exquisite and elaborate works of art and craftsmanship. The people speak English, but their writing is totally different from English script or printing, and Smith has to be taught to read the magnificently illuminated volumes which recount their history and beliefs. The House is ruled by a Father, the only bearded man of the community, who is said to be almost two hundred years old.

Smith learns that the whole world is now possessed only by widely separated comparable houses that are known to one another from the reports of pilgrims. Belatedly, Smith finds that there is also a Mother, the real ruler and principal person of the community. The reader, rather than Smith, comes to see that sexuality is absent from this society except for the Father and the Mother, who alone have the responsibility of perpetuating it. Except for these two, sexual love is replaced by kindliness, by creation of things of beauty, and by reverent enjoyment of the beauty of the earth and cultivation of its fruits. Smith is constantly embarrassed by his blunders, and constantly he more deeply and passionately loves the girl Yoletta—who he learns is a woman of thirty-one.

As the book nears its end, the reader gradually perceives that the Mother, Chastel, who is very ill—in marked contrast to the perfect health of the other members of the community—has taken a special interest in Smith and that he is under consideration as a new Father of the House, with Yoletta as the Mother and his bride. But, even as Smith glimpses this prospect, he is reading ancient books of the community that cause him to have a profound desire to wipe from his memory all that remains of his earlier life and all that he has known before entering the Crystal Age. When, as result, he drinks the liquid in a flask labeled "Drink of me and be cured," he dies.

A *Crystal Age* draws its not inconsiderable dramatic strength from the characterization of Smith, who is sufficiently consistent as an ordinary modern Englishman in his bewilderments, blunders, and passion for Yoletta, as well as in his schemings and his bafflements, to gain a substantial measure of empathy. There is a measure of dramatic reality also in the Father and a large measure in the Mother, Chastel, in her physical suffering and in her gradually developing interest in Smith after she learns that, with his hand on her forehead, she can sleep. In some measure recognizably human and alive also is Edra—the friend and mentor of Yoletta—and Yoletta herself; the other members of the community (who number only a dozen or so) are colorless and undifferentiated.

The whole effect of the book, obviously, is to project against the mass misery, frustration, and futility of the modern world, which are concretely realized in the thoughts and conduct of Smith, the vision of human beings living in complete harmony with the earth and with each other. Some years after the publication of A *Crystal Age,* Hudson defended certain aspects of the book in a letter of August 17, 1893, to an American friend, Louise Chandler Moulton, who had apparently objected to the death of Smith and also to the characterization of Chastel as inconsistent with the general pattern of life in *The Crystal Age:*

You are keenly appreciative of whatever is good in the book, & kindly say nothing of its faults, which are not few. But about poor Smith, what was to be done with him? He, a commonplace, modern, "bank-holiday sort of young man" could never have got himself into any sort of harmony with that serene passionless social atmosphere into which he was thrown. It was better that he should die accidentally and escape from a false position. And as for Chastel: well, I could do nothing with those quiet-minded humans of the future, they seemed so unlike ourselves, & so was obliged to introduce one tempestuous pain-racked soul to preserve something of human interest in the narrative.[9]

Stylistically, *A Crystal Age* is as distinctive as its material. There are long passages, especially in speeches of the Father, which are marked by a Ruskin-like eloquence of great beauty. Other passages of natural description are akin to Hudson's most characteristic in later writings, recording his own actual experience, in their power and beauty.

A Crystal Age owes little to its immediate predecessors in the history of utopian romance. The immediate suggestion for such a work may have come from Richard Jefferies' *After London* (1885), for Hudson knew and admired Jefferies' books about nature. But *After London* has nothing in texture or substance to align it with Hudson's work. The widely read *Erewhon* (1872) of Samuel Butler is a more probable source, for in *Erewhon,* as in *A Crystal Age,* sickness is a crime that is punishable—though the correlated idea, that crime is an illness and is to be given sympathetic medical treatment—is not suggested at all. Moreover, *A Crystal Age* has not the slightest suggestion of the savage irony of Butler's treatment of religious and educational institutions.

A Crystal Age is wholly antithetical to the most popular of the utopian romances which succeeded it, Edward Bellamy's *Looking Backward* (1888), in which machinery, which has been destroyed or reduced to the simple forms of a primitive plow and an ax in *A Crystal Age,* has become the means of solving the material problems of man and of freeing him for the development of his intellect and soul. Hudson's romance also has nothing of the intention of immediate social criticism and commentary which mark either Bellamy's work or William Dean Howells' *A Traveler from Altruria* (1894) and his *Through the Eye of the Needle* (1907). *The Crystal Age* is most closely approached in structure, in tone, in the nature of the utopia described, and in style, by William Morris' *News from Nowhere* (1891), and I think it wholly probable that Morris knew Hudson's book.

Lewis Mumford has made in his *The Story of the Utopias* the most discerning comment on *A Crystal Age* that work has yet received. He sees that the most significant literary relationship of *A Crystal Age* is to the original *Utopia* of Sir Thomas More: "Mr. W. H. Hudson returns upon More; and in *A Crystal Age* the farmstead and the family is the ultimate unit of social life."[10] Mumford also defines clearly the biological concept which underlies the picture of society presented by Hudson: a single female, the Mother, is chosen for the sole function of reproduction and the perpetuation of the family; and a single male is likewise selected as her mate:

To the objection that this sort of utopia requires that we change human nature, the answer, in terms of modern biology, is that there is no apparent scientific reason why certain elements in human nature should not be selected and brought to the front, or why certain others should not be reduced in importance and eliminated. So, for all practical purposes, there is no apparent reason why human nature should not be changed, or why we should not be prepared to believe that in times past it has been changed . . . a utopia which rests upon the notion that there should be a certain direction in our breeding is not altogether luny; indeed, is nowadays less so than ever before, for the reason that it is possible to separate romantic love from physical procreation without, as the Athenians did, resorting to homosexuality.

If *A Crystal Age* opens our minds to these possibilities, it is not to be counted purely as a romance, in spite of the fact that as a romance it has passages that rival *Green Mansions*. Between the individual households and common marriages, the utopia of the beehive is a third alternative which possibly remains to be explored.[11]

Mumford's analysis of the central idea in *A Crystal Age* is confirmed by a passage in a letter of June 10, 1917, from Hudson to Edward Garnett, in which he said: "The sexual passion is the central thought in the *Crystal Age:* the idea that there is no millennium, no rest, no perpetual peace till that fury has burnt itself out, and I gave unlimited time for the change. It is . . . the social model of the beehive with the queen mother in its centre."[12] Because of this letter's statement about the beehive and the queen mother, the initial conception of *A Crystal Age* may have come from a passage in Thomas Belt's *The Naturalist in Nicaragua* (1874), which was well known to Hudson. It is cited more frequently in Hudson's own first book of essays on nature, *The Naturalist in La Plata* (1892) than any other recent scientific work except Darwin's—and Belt's ideas are always given approval. Belt, after commenting on his observations on the conduct of several species of communal ants (similar to that of bees), enumerates in detail the aspects of their behavior which are strikingly illustrative of coöperation and fruitful community action. He then quotes at length from Sir Thomas More's *Utopia* his account of a reformed human society: "there is no unequal distribution, so that no man is poor nor in any necessity, and though no man has anything, yet they are all rich. . . ."[13] Belt's comparison of an insect society with the human, to the discredit of the latter, and especially his quotation from More, justify the suggestion that this message may have influenced, or even initiated, Hudson's conception of the society pictured in *A Crystal Age*.

It remains to note the significance of *A Crystal Age* as expressive of Hudson's religious view and position. Although the relatively limited critical writing about Hudson includes various attempts to define his religious position, with much employment of such terms as animism, Hudson's religion was actually relatively simple; it is clearly expressed in and through the whole body of his work. It was earth worship: reverence and sympathy for every form of life and for all living things, reverence for the earth itself as the source and sustainer of all life, and reverent acceptance of the conditions and limitations of the life of every creature. This religion is also that of the people of *The Crystal Age*, as it is revealed through the imperfect and gradual perception of Smith.

III Fan

Fan, Hudson's third novel, was published in 1892 under the pseudonym of "Henry Harford." It was not merely the concealed authorship which prevented *Fan* from contributing to Hudson's dawning reputation. The book shows strong influence from contemporary sentimental and romantic best sellers, if not indeed a conscious or unconscious imitation of these in character and action. Perhaps the most charitable judgment is to view the book as Hudson's attempt, out of the extreme poverty and hardship of the years in London following his marriage, to gain a share of the financial rewards so liberally extended to the authors of some of these works.

Fan herself, the central character of the book, is an extreme example of the mistreated heroine of sentimental fiction: at fifteen, the only environment she has known is that of the London slums; the only intimate human relations, those with her drunken

mother, who is killed in a brawl with another woman at the outset of the story, and with a brutal foster-father who deserts her.
Briefly sheltered by kindly women of the slums but with no
prospect of escape from abject poverty, Fan is rescued by Miss
Starbrow, a brilliant, selfish, and impulsive woman who takes a
fancy to her and who places her in the home of a clergyman in
a country village for tutoring. There she becomes the bone of con-
tention between her two feminine tutors, survives a violent ab-
duction and threat of rape, is loved by and loves a young man
who turns out to be her half-brother, and is finally shown to be
the illegitimate daughter of a gentleman—which is apparently
meant to account for the fine qualities of her mind and nature.
In broad outline, *Fan* is, therefore, a preposterous and sentimental story; to this degree, it deserved the contempt, silent or
expressed, with which most readers of Hudson have treated it.
The pitiless but just review given it by one contemporary periodical expressed the hope that what "appears to be its author's
first experiment in fiction . . . may also prove his last. . . ."[14]

But *Fan* deserves attention from the serious student of Hudson
because of some of its positive qualities. Among these is the
graphic rendering of life in the slums, which may well draw its
convincingness from Hudson's own experience in his early years
of extreme poverty in London. Other substantial lines of interest
are those provided by the development of the religious and
economic conflicts of the time, which are dramatized in the
conduct and conversation of rather firmly realized and convincing characters. For, when Fan is placed in a rectory in a rural
village for a year's tutoring, her experience there includes a bitter
conflict between two older women, the wife and the daughter
of the rector, for control of her religious life. The mother is an
arrogant and intolerant traditionalist; the daughter, a freethinker.
Similarly, when Fan later goes to London and becomes a wage
earner there, her association with a young reform journalist and
his wife gives opportunity for concrete dramatization of social
and economic conflict.

Apart from these elements, both all but unique in Hudson,
the most interesting aspect of the novel is the attempt to drama-
tize in Fan herself something of Hudson's own feeling for life
and living things: his earth worship. The first fully developed
incident of the book is Fan's solitary expedition, despite her

mother's opposition, to the countryside near London where she hopes to see something of the beauty of fields and woodlands of which she has read. The incident is intrinsically unconvincing, but the treatment is strongly realistic. Fan walks for miles until she is tired, and then it begins to rain: "The few trees visible were bare of foliage, and the fields, shut within their brown ragged hedges, were mostly ploughed and black, and the green fields were as level as the ploughed, and there was no shelter from the cold wind, no sunshine on the damp sward."[14] Fan finds at last a nest in some dry leaves under an oak tree, rests and falls asleep, and then, deeply disappointed, makes her way back to the slums.

When Fan is rescued by Miss Starbrow, she responds eagerly to the beauty of the lady's garden. Later, in the village, her enjoyment of flowers and of the beauty of fields and woods is extensively developed. Perhaps the best example, highly characteristic of Hudson, is the account of her experience of "the songs of innumerable birds":

Loud and close at hand were heard the lusty notes of thrush and blackbird, chaffinch and blackcap; and from these there was a gradation of sounds, down to the faint lispings of the more tender melodists singing at a distance, reaching the sense like voices mysterious and spiritualized from some far unseen world. And at intervals came the fluting cry of the cuckoo, again and again repeated, so aerial, yet with such a passionate depth in it, as if the Spirit of Nature itself had become embodied, and from some leafy hiding-place cried aloud with mystic lips.[15]

Tone and substance and the comparable passages about nature would identify this novel, so alien in many ways, as indeed the work of W. H. Hudson.

IV Tales of the Pampas

Hudson's best short fiction, collected under the title *El Ombú*, was first published in 1902 by the London firm of Duckworth and Company. The book was accepted because of the enthusiasm of Edward Garnett, who had just become Duckworth's reader. A lifelong friendship which resulted led to the series of letters from Hudson to Garnett which, with the letters to Morley Roberts, constitute our most valuable biographical and personal

revelation of Hudson's later life.[16] Duckworth published the
volume again in 1909, with no changes in the text but with a
new title, *South American Sketches*. When the success of *Green
Mansions* created a demand for Hudson's work in the United
States, Alfred A. Knopf brought out the volume under still a
third and a better title, *Tales of the Pampas* (1916), adding to
it a very early, inferior, and previously uncollected story and
also a long narrative poem.

Of the four stories included in the two Duckworth editions,
"The Story of a Piebald Horse" was an unintegrated chapter
taken from *The Purple Land;* the story of a mysterious disappearance in the violent pampas life is explained by a first-person
narrative: the family of the man who has disappeared cause his
piebald horse to be kept tethered at a wayside tavern, and eventually a man who recognizes the horse appears and tells the
story which explains the mystery. "Nino Diablo" is marked by
humor of a high order and by strong suspense. The widely
feared killer and outlaw, the *nino diablo*, is appealed to by a
despairing rancher whose wife has been captured by Indians;
later, he listens unrecognized to the abuse and threats uttered
against him by another visitor to the same *estancia*. He steals
the braggart's horses and succeeds in rescuing the rancher's wife.

The major achievement of the volume is found in the two
longer stories—the title story and "Martha Riquelme." "El Ombú"
is a story told in the first person, with a single brief introductory
paragraph:

This history of a house that had been was told in the shade, one summer's day, by Nicandro, that old man to whom we all loved to listen,
since he could remember and properly narrate the life of every person
he had known in his native place, near to the lake of Chascomus, on
the southern pampas of Buenos Ayres.[17]

The narrative which follows—one of violence, death, insanity, and
love—is perfectly controlled and integrated by the quiet, slightly
formal, explicit style of the narrator. Its effect is one of massive-
ness; of intense human experience rendered only the more poignant by the narrator's consistent simplicity and understatement.
Few works of fiction of comparable length, in English or in any
other literature, equal it in essential power or in completeness
of achievement.

In the first paragraph Hudson sketches swiftly, with details which remain in the reader's memory as background until the end of the story, the physical setting as it is at the time of Nicandro's recital of the people and events associated with the place:

In all this district, though you should go twenty leagues to this way and that, you will not find a tree as big as this ombú, standing solitary, where there is no house; therefore it is known to all as "*the* ombú," as if but one existed; and the name of all this estate, which is now owner-less and ruined, is El Ombú. From one of the higher branches, if you can climb, you will see the lake of Chascomus, two thirds of a league away, from shore to shore, and the village on its banks. Even smaller things will you see on a clear day; perhaps a red line moving across the water—a flock of flamingos flying in their usual way. A great tree standing alone, with no house near it; only the old brick foundations of a house, so overgrown with grass and weeds that you have to look closely to find them. When I am out with my flock in the summer time, I often come here to sit in the shade.[18]

Nicandro first tells the story of Don Santos Ugarte, an early owner of the *estancia* called El Ombú because of its one enor-mous ombú tree (like the twenty-five of Hudson's first home), which is visible for many miles. Ugarte, who is known to be the father of many sons in the neighborhood, is ironically unable to have a son of his own name though he has three times mar-ried. When a slave, an intelligent and gentle boy who has been especially favored by Ugarte, saves his money until he has enough to buy his freedom and offers it to Ugarte, his master kills him, goes into self-imposed exile to escape punishment, and never returns to the estate. He dies, an old man, as a suicide by drowning.

Nicandro then turns to the story of more recent occupants of the *estancia*, Nicandro's beloved friend, Valerio, and his family. Valerio has a happy marriage and an idolized little son, Bruno. Both Nicandro and Valerio are conscripted to serve in the forces of one Colonel Barboza. When the troops are discharged, Bar-boza cheats them of their pay, and Valerio is chosen to present a protest. Barboza first sentences him to be flayed alive but then reduces the punishment to two hundred lashes. Valerio, all but killed by the flogging, is conducted back to El Ombú by

Nicandro, but he dies as he is being greeted by his wife and child.

The widowed mother, Donata, takes into her arms a deserted child, a girl named Monica, who grows up with Bruno. She is very beautiful, kind, and gentle, and the two learn to love each other. But, when he is grown, Bruno learns for the first time the circumstances of his father's death; and, in spite of Nicandro's efforts to dissuade him, leaves secretly with the purpose of revenge, and all efforts to find him fail. Donata takes into her house at El Ombú a penniless and dispossessed old couple; shortly thereafter she dies, leaving Monica with them. Monica rejects all suitors, waiting for Bruno's return.

After years, a returning soldier tells Nicandro and Monica of the final insanity and strange death of Barboza, following an attempt to assassinate him in which he kills the would-be assassin. At the end of his story, he names as an afterthought the man who had tried to kill Barboza—Bruno de la Cueva. On hearing these words, Monica falls senseless to the floor, and thereafter she has no memory and no reason. When the old house at El Ombú is torn down "for the sake of the material which was required for a building in the village,"[19] Monica is taken by the old woman whom Donata had befriended to live with relatives at a nearby town, and she remains with them after the old woman's death. The people of the town "are kind to her," Nicandro says, "for her story is known to them, and God has put compassion into their hearts."[20]

The final paragraph of Nicandro's narrative illustrates the concreteness, the simplicity, and the tinge of formality which mark Hudson's style and tone of the narrative:

To see her you would hardly believe that she is the Monica I have told you of, whom I knew as a little one, running barefoot after her father's flock. For she has grey hairs and wrinkles now. As you ride to Chascomus from this point you will see, on approaching the lake, a very high bank on your left hand, covered with a growth of tall fennel, hoarhound, and cardoon thistle. There on most days you will find her, sitting on the bank in the shade of the tall fennel bushes, looking across the lake. She watches for the flamingos. There are many of those great birds on the lake, and they go in flocks, and when they rise and travel across the water, flying low, their scarlet wings may be seen at a great distance. And every time she catches sight of a flock moving like

a red line across the lake she cries out with delight. That is her one
happiness—her life. And she is the last of all those who have lived in my
time at El Ombú.[21]

In some ways even more remarkable is the other long story,
"Marta Riquelme," which was first published in the edition of
1902. It is told in the first person by a Roman Catholic missionary
who is sent to a remote village at the foot of the Andes, where
the people, nominally converted, are actually still under the
dominion of the ancient heathen gods. The young cleric, struggling against himself, falls in love with a girl of Spanish blood
whose name gives the story its title; and he watches her tragic
life until she becomes at last a *Kakue*, a birdlike demon of the
forest. Because of the agony resulting from his witnessing this
transformation, the narrator returns to Spain, to his beloved
Córdoba, expecting to die there. Instead, he regains his health
and is sent again to the remote village of his earlier ministry,
where he finally regains a measure of his former faith.

The narrative is as consistent in its integrity of revelation as is
that of "El Ombú"; but the essential intent of "Marta Riquelme"
is that of swiftly intensifying psychological anguish. The very
firm specification of place and character in the earlier part of
the story makes inevitable the reader's extreme measure of participation in the climax of Martha's agony and in that of the
priest when she rejects the crucifix and is claimed by the powers
of evil. Narrower in its emotional range than "El Ombú" and
perhaps less within the emotional grasp of some readers, "Marta
Riquelme" is another great story and one that is all but unique
for Hudson in its psychological realism.

As was suggested at the beginning of this discussion, the two
items added to the original group in *Tales of the Pampas* (1916)
are far inferior to the four of the earlier collection. They are a
prose narrative, some forty pages in length, entitled "Pelino
Viera's Confession"; the fortunately shorter narrative in verse is
"Tecla and the Little Men." Both are frankly supernatural in
material. Neither constitutes an addition of value to the earlier
volume or to Hudson's literary achievement.

V   Green Mansions

Green Mansions, Hudson's fifth book of fiction, gained mod-

erate success upon its publication in England in 1904; and it was
highly praised by discriminating readers. Not until more than a
decade later, however, did an enterprising and able young
American publisher, Alfred A. Knopf, obtain rights for the publication in the United States and, by his personal enthusiasm
and skillful advertising, catapult the novel into best-sellerdom
and earn for Hudson the first real financial success he had ever
known. *Green Mansions* remains the only book of Hudson's
widely recognized in the literary world. If we mention W. H.
Hudson, the response is almost certain to be: "Ah yes, the *Green
Mansions* man."

Hudson himself said that the story was awkwardly told and
moved too slowly. In his excellent introduction to the novel,
Carlos Baker quotes Hudson as declaring: "All through the story
is told in a leisurely way and very minutely, but the introductory
chapters seem too slow; the story . . . simply sits still and stews
contentedly in its own juice, . . . like a saucepot of cocoa-nibs that
has all the day before it."[22] Professor Baker also notes the resemblance of Hudson's method in *Green Mansions* to Joseph
Conrad's favorite way of introducing a novel.[23] In a "prologue"
we are given an account of the central character, Mr. Abel, as a
man of unknown background living in Georgetown, British
Guiana, and of his friendship with the first-person speaker in the
prologue. The prologue includes reference to Mr. Abel's recent
death and to a cinerary urn, strangely ornamented and inscribed,
found among his effects. The speaker of the prologue then tells
of his reproaching Mr. Abel for the latter's total lack of revelation
of his past life. The novel proper consists of the story told by
Mr. Abel in response to this challenge.

Fleeing from political turmoil in Venezuela and the probability
of execution, Abel travels far into remote jungle areas. Passing
from one tribe of Indians to another, he undergoes a severe
illness, hunts fruitlessly for gold, at last settles with a small group
of Indians whose chieftain is called Runi. As his health gradually
returns. Abel begins to explore the hunting grounds of Runi's
tribe; and he discovers that one area of forest, though near and
promising, is forbidden. The Indians are afraid to enter it, be-
lieving it is the domain of an evil spirit, "the daughter of the
Didi." When Abel disregards their warnings and enters this forest,
he hears "a low strain of exquisite bird-melody, wonderfully pure

and expressive, unlike any musical sound I had ever heard before."[24]

Disregarding the warnings of his Indian hosts, he returns again and again to the forbidden forest; and at last he sees and speaks with a beautiful girl, Rima, who is the source of the mysterious voice. Gradually Abel gains her confidence and discovers that she lives alone with an old man named Ruflo in a hidden spot in the forest. Rima speaks Spanish, but by preference she uses another language totally unknown to Abel. She wears a dress of her own handiwork made from cobwebs. Utterly fascinated by her strange beauty, by her knowledge, and by her power in the jungle, Abel falls very deeply in love with her, and he finally submits to her ardent wish to make a long journey to the land where she has been born and where her mother has died.

The hard journey is made by Rima, Abel, and Ruflo; only at its end is Rima convinced that she cannot find her people. In the extremity of this disappointment, she realizes her love for Abel and her dependence on him, but she insists on returning to her beloved forest as swiftly as she can—far more quickly than Abel and Ruflo can travel. When, after an exhausting journey, Abel returns to the forest, he finds Ruflo's hut destroyed; later he encounters his savage former hosts hunting in the once forbidden forest. Shortly, he learns that they have killed Rima by burning a tree in which she had taken refuge. Abel remains in the jungle long enough to collect her ashes and to avenge her death by killing her murderers; he then undergoes great hardship, nears death, and eventually returns to civilization.

What in *Green Mansions* gave the book its strong and lasting appeal, making it one of the most widely read and loved novels of its time? A partial answer lies in the powerful characterization of Abel, the narrator and dramatic center of the story—in the extraordinary "solidity of specification" with which he is portrayed. He is vain, crafty, curious, brave, vengeful, capable of deep love and murderous hate; in short, he is thoroughly human. Without his richly achieved perspective, the all-but-supernatural character of Rima as first seen would be rejected as incredible; and her gradual transformation and growth from a child of nature to a woman ready for love would have little chance of being convincing. The final forty pages of the novel—

narrating Abel's discovery of Rima's death, his revenge, and the periods of near starvation, illness, despair, and partial insanity which he undergoes—reinforce and are consistent with the earlier characterization of him.

Matching the reality of Abel is Hudson's achievement in establishing the tropical setting. He is sparing (in comparison to the essays) in his use of specific details of tree, shrub, flower, bird, reptile; but, whenever dramatic incident depends on precise detail—as in the incident of Abel's being bitten by a deadly coral snake—the detail is brilliant. Indeed, the whole achievement of the novel rests ultimately on its stylistic excellence—its unfailingly consistent unobtrusive concreteness, its richness of cadence, and its responsiveness in sound and rhythm to content. Always subdued to its narrative purpose, the style never obtrudes itself on the reader's attention; yet it never fails to maintain his interest. It is almost as difficult to find in the whole texture of the novel a sentence outstanding in its excellence, and so distinguished from its neighbors, as it is to find one in any significant way inferior.

Adverse criticism of *Green Mansions* is usually focused on the characterization of Rima. Representative and exceptionally sweeping is that of Hoxie N. Fairchild, who in an article on Hudson's sources for the novel confesses to "a lively distaste for Rima"; he asserts that "one cannot believe in her as anything" and calls her "Too avian to be human and too human to be preternatural, too unearthly to be a woman and too womanly to be a bird. . . ."[25] In his indictment Fairchild ignores the fact that, from first to last, we see Rima only through Abel's eyes. To him, and to us as readers, she is at first wholly mystifying. Her uncanny ability to escape Abel's vision, her ability to travel through treetops, and her birdlike voice are inexplicable. But gradually, with Abel, we see the woman in her emerge: in her anger at Abel's attempt to kill the coral snake, in her slowly responding awareness of Abel's love for her and in her attraction toward him, in her abuse of old Ruflo and in her transformations when she is in the hut and out of the forest, in her imperious will and in her collapse at its frustration she is thoroughly human. Her womanliness is finally fully revealed in her response of awakened love when she finds herself in Abel's arms at the cave at Riolama. The ultimate decisive detail is her urgency to depart from Riolama, so that she can have time to prepare a new garment for herself—a worthy garment for her wedding.

Rima's garment, made of cobwebs, is sometimes cited as a detail that is unconvincing. Curiously, this detail finds documentation as to its possibility in Hudson's first published writings. In his letter of March 22, 1870, to Dr. P. L. Sclater of the London Zoological Society, Hudson reports his observation, beside a stream, of a "zone of gossamer . . . about twenty yards wide" and two miles long that was composed of the accumulated webs of innumerable spiders. He adds: "I enclose you a small strip of the webs that could be easily peeled off of every object presenting a smooth surface." The possibility of a fabric composed of cobwebs was not, therefore, a fanciful invention, but a product of Hudson's own experience.

Nor is Rima herself so romantically conceived as to be beyond the acceptance of a multitude of readers. In her small size and with her birdlike voice, she, as Ford Madox Ford contended, suggests Hudson's own tiny wife.[27] In her protective love of all things in nature—even of a deadly coral snake—her attitude is simply Hudson's own actual position. Relatively few readers, and those unfortunate, fail to find in their own experience some trace of an idealizing love akin to Abel's, however "romantic" our adult view may see it to be. The great and enduring appeal of *Green Mansions* rests, in part, on this all-but-universal experience; in part, on its brilliantly rendered exotic background; and, in part, as already suggested, on the power and precision of the wholly human character of Abel.

Perhaps there is a deeper reason for the wide appreciation of *Green Mansions,* one not consciously recognized by most readers. It is Hudson's supreme dramatic expression of his recognition of the mystery of life: the mystery of death as an inseparable part of life, of all birth and growing and flowering, of all beauty, all happiness, and all achievement. This recognition is present in all his work, but it is more often glimpsed or implied than overtly expressed—the quality which ultimately distinguishes him, perhaps, from lesser writers. Hudson's recognition of the ultimate mystery of life is classical rather than romantic; and, though *Green Mansions* may perhaps justifiably be called a romantic novel—if only for the demands it makes on our imaginations— these is no romantic cloudiness in its ultimate meaning.

Green Mansions has also been a happy hunting ground for critics and scholars interested in sources and influences. As to the character of Rima, an early critic, Henry S. Salt, pointed out her resemblance to Miranda, the heroine of Charles G. D. Roberts' *The Heart of the Ancient Wood*. Miranda, growing up alone with her mother in a remote clearing in the Canadian wilderness, achieves a communion much like Rima's with nature, as well as friendship with all living things. An amusing parallel between the novels may be noted in old Ruflo's secrecy in eating meat— forbidden by Rima—and the success of the young hunter who is Miranda's lover in his prescription of fried venison for her mother's illness. The endings of the two novels, however, are antithetical: Miranda achieves at the end a total "return to the human," even to the extent of shooting with somewhat incredible accuracy her beloved old she-bear, to save the life of her lover; but Rima dies in the great fire kindled by the savages.

The suggestion of Roberts' book as a source gains credibility from Hudson's admiration for Roberts' writing as a whole. In one of his last books, *A Traveller in Little Things*, Hudson mentions "Charles Roberts, the Canadian" as "no doubt the greatest" of "several writers on animals who are not exactly naturalists, nor yet mere fictionists, but who, to a considerable knowledge of animal psychology and extraordinary sympathy with all wildness, unite an imaginative insight which reveals to them much of the inner, the mind life of brutes."[28]

Hoxie N. Fairchild argues vigorously for the provenance of the figure of Rima in a poem by Arthur O'Shaughnessy, "Colibri," in *Songs of a Worker* (1881).[29] Another suggestion as to the origin of Hudson's conception of Rima is Lady Morgan in Sidney Owenson's novel *The Missionary* (1811), which has been advanced by Carlos Baker in his introduction to *Green Mansions*.[30]

More important for the student of Hudson than any fictional archetypes of Rima, however, is the relationship of Hudson's novel to certain works of travel and description of the upper Amazon region which were available to him; for, it is an astonishing fact, Hudson had never visited the part of South America which he describes so frequently and so vividly with so much detail in *Green Mansions*. He drew both general impressions of the upper Amazon country and the borders of Venezuela and British Guiana, which form the background of

Green Mansions, and details of plants, animals, and human inhabitants, from the works of firsthand observers. Certainly among
these was H. W. Bates's *The Naturalist on the River Amazons*
(1864), which Hudson is known to have read and admired and
which is rich in notation of fauna and flora. Bates spent eleven
years in scientific collecting expeditions in the region of the
Amazon and its tributaries and brought back—according to Darwin, in his appreciative comment on Bates's work—specimens of
about eight-thousand species "previously unknown to science."

An important factor in Hudson's effective technique in *Green
Mansions* is his steady reliance on concrete details of Abel's
actual physical experience to anchor the at first inexplicable
and near-incredible presentation of Rima. From Abel's first en-
trance into the forbidden forest that is Rima's domain, the reader
sees through his eyes (and hears through his ears) a consistent
succession of plants, birds, insects, and animals which ground
the narrative firmly in objective reality. Within a dozen pages,
in Abel's first visit to Rima's domain, we see and hear vividly
at least a dozen outstanding details of the environment; and
this method is maintained, although the details become less numerous as the narrative progresses, are more fully developed and
even dramatized, as in the case of the coral snake which Rima
befriends but which bites Abel, and that of the sloth which he
kills near the end of the jungle experience. There is no doubt
that many or most of these details of the life of a region which
Hudson had not himself visited came from those in Bates's book.

Other probable sources for realistic details of jungle life, natural and human, in a region not included in Hudson's own experience, are Alfred Simson's, *Travels in the Wilds of Ecuador*
(1886), noted by Baker,[31] and Everard F. im Thurn's *Among
the Indians of Guiana* (1883). Either may have suggested the
place name of Riolama, the unreached goal of the pilgrimage of
Rima, Abel, and Ruflo, since both contain names suggestive of
it; im Thurn's book is primarily anthropological, as its title suggests, and it offers many details paralleled in *Green Mansions.*
In further support of the probability that *Among the Indians
of Guiana* was a source for *Green Mansions* is the fact that it is
quoted extensively in Hudson's first collection of essays on nature,
The Naturalist in La Plata (1893).

VI　A Little Boy Lost

A Little Boy Lost, which appeared in the year following *Green Mansions* (1905), has received scant notice from critics, who dismiss it as a book for children; but it repays closer inspection. In its earliest chapters, *A Little Boy Lost* is firmly anchored to Hudson's own earliest experience. The little boy's parents live in an isolated home on the pampas; the child's gradual exploration of his immediate surroundings closely parallels the earliest experience narrated in *Far Away and Long Ago;* and the details— the trees, the stream, the birds—are identical. The little boy, like his creator, loves all living things, alarms his parents by bringing a snake into the house; he is heartbroken when unintentionally he kills a spoonbill—a bird admired by the boy of *Far Away and Long Ago.* The plants familiar to the reader of that book are in these early chapters too, notably the giant thistles.

Martin, the little boy of the story, unlike his creator, runs away from home and is lost while pursuing visionary people of the mirage. In a dream, he sees these people—a wounded young man of great beauty and a gracious queen. He is found and taken to his hut by a deaf old rancher who bears a strong family resemblance to some of the neighbors described in *Far Away and Long Ago.* Threatened with a beating, Martin escapes from the hut in the night. Shortly he falls in with a small band of savages (first cousins to those described in *Green Mansions*) who tolerate his presence with them kindly enough but do not interfere when their children steal his clothes, leaving him naked. He wanders through a forest reminiscent of that in *Green Mansions,* encountering animals and plants realistically described, and he undergoes two strange adventures.

In the first, which is essentially comic, the boy wakens from sleep to find himself surrounded by a group of old men in long black coats, whose behavior is both timid and threatening, and who turn out to be vultures who fly away when he shows that he is alive. In the second, he encounters a troop of wild horses controlled by a naked wild man who seizes Martin, tries to teach him to eat grass as the man himself does, and then feeds him mare's milk. Martin escapes by falling from his mount in a vast growth of tall reeds, a familiar place to Hudson readers.

After this adventure, the book veers toward a conventional fairy-tale plot. Martin is rescued by a lovely Lady of the Hills, who comforts and cares for him. Beautiful clothing is made for him in a subterranean workshop by dwarfs who bear a strong resemblance to the elves of tradition. But, though treated with affection, Martin is obsessed by a desire to see the great blue water which he has heard lies beyond the hills. The Lady of the Hills warns him against it and tries to keep him with her, but he breaks away and finally reaches the ocean. Here he is enchanted by the blueness and space; but he finds the waves, when he actually encounters them, rough playfellows. He gains refuge on an ancient raft; he is seen and circled over by enormous flocks of birds; as a result, he is observed from a passing sailing ship; and the book ends abruptly.

Perhaps the tale of Martin's adventures resembles imaginings of the very youthful Hudson as he played on the great plain around his home and wondered what lay beyond the horizon. Certainly actual experiences of that child of long ago are to be found in the texture of the story. Closely read, it parallels in inner meaning the grim parable of *Green Mansions* and the ultimate frustration of a search for the ideal.

VII *"Dead Man's Plack" and "An Old Thorn"*

Two widely divergent stories of greatly unequal length, published with their combined titles in 1920, are products of the last years of Hudson's life. "Dead Man's Plack" begins with a lengthy Preamble in which Hudson amusingly and effectively attacks the methods and conclusions of the eminent British historian E. A. Freeman, and, through him, all scholarly pretentiousness and dogmatism. Hudson tells how he found in his rambling in Hampshire a beautiful stone cross which purports to mark the spot where King Edgar of England killed his friend and favorite, Earl Athelwold, because the friend had deceived him about the beauty of Elfrida—declaring her homely—and had then married her himself. After the death of Athelwold, Edgar ultimately made her his queen. Hudson shows how Freeman bungled in condemning the old story of the cross as false and then refused to admit his mistake.

From this Preamble Hudson proceeds to a retelling of the ancient story. Gradually, the focus is narrowed to Elfrida herself; and the story becomes one of searching psychological realism that is told against a vivid background of the bloody struggle for power in the infant English nation. The story is told with the powerful simplicity that marks Hudson's mature style, and the tale achieves rich realization of the part played by religion and religious institutions in the life of the times. Perhaps some readers have been repelled by this dark and bloody tale because they found in it so little of what is most often valued in Hudson's work. Indeed, it is unique in the whole body of his writing in its choice of historical material and in its central focus on the fact and the effect of sin as a reality in human life. In a brief postscript, Hudson confesses that he has not penetrated the ultimate depths of Elfrida's experience or professed to know the whole truth about her. But, for the reader who is willing to share in this unique experiment of a great writer, "Dead Man's Plack" is a rich and unforgettable reading experience.

The much shorter "An Old Thorn" has a closer relationship to the main body of Hudson's writing than the study of Elfrida. Indeed, in a note about the story at the end of the volume, Hudson refers the reader to passages in *A Shepherd's Life* which deal with the extreme cruelty of the sentences dealt out to rural people convicted of stealing sheep and other comparable offenses, in the late eighteenth and early nineteenth centuries in England. The story is essentially an account of such a crime—committed by one Johnnie Budd to save a wife and children from starvation—and of the trial, conviction, and sentence of death which followed. What distinguishes the story, and highly, is the part played in it by an ancient thorn tree, topped with ivy. Hudson first describes the tree vividly, then tells how he is thwarted in all his attempts to gain information about the tree from the villagers of the neighborhood. Then he tells the story of Johnnie Budd and the part played in his life by the tree.

As Johnnie is being taken in a cart, handcuffed, to his trial, with almost certain condemnation to death before him, he pleads with the constable to stop and to let him stand for one minute under the old thorn tree. The constable, who is reluctant, is rebuked by an old man who is driving the cart; and Johnnie has his wish. As a child he had injured the tree by climbing it and had been warned by a mysterious stranger who came riding by that the tree would never forgive him. Now he kneels and presses his face against the tree, murmuring to it. Thereafter, he is patient and resigned, meeting his sentence without complaint.

From the story emerges a glimpse of a conception of a tree as a decisive power in human lives. In a note at the end of the book, Hudson remarks that the story—historically true—"is the only narrative I know of dealing with that rare and curious subject, the survival of tree-worship in our own country."[32] In its union of this deep and strange conception with the simple and tender treatment of Johnnie's life and death, "An Old Thorn" is one of Hudson's finest and most memorable stories.

When *Dead Man's Plack and An Old Thorn* was republished in 1924, five poems were added to the volume. These included "Tecla and the Little Men," previously noted in connection with *El Ombú;* "The London Sparrow"; "In the Wilderness"; "Gwendoline"; and "The Old Man in Kensington Gardens." All are of negligible merit and, as a whole, they add nothing to Hudson's achievement as a writer. However, the final lines of "The London Sparrow" (which according to the publisher's statement first appeared in a periodical called *Merry England* in the 1880's) are noteworthy for a powerful statement of an aspect of Hudson's view of human life on the earth as transient, doomed to end (at least in the cities) which is elsewhere encountered chiefly in his final books:

> So, gleaner unregarded, flittest thou
> Now, as of old, and in the years to come,
> Nature's one witness, till the murmuring sound
> Of human feet unnumbered, like the rain
> Of summer pattering on the forest leaves,
> Fainter and fainter falling midst the ruin,
> In everlasting silence dies away.[33]

VIII   Ralph Herne

Ralph Herne, the last of Hudson's longer fiction to find book publication (1923), was perhaps the first in order of composition. Although I believe that it may have been written, at least in a partial draft, before Hudson left South America in 1874, it appeared in 1888 as a serial in a magazine called *Youth.* It is the story of a young Englishman, orphaned and poor, who is helped

to a medical education in England by a benefactor but cannot
afford to buy into a practice. He goes as a ship's doctor to Buenos
Aires and decides to settle there, but he is denied certification
in spite of his record in England. He fails in an examination,
becomes dissipated, plays cards, and loses all his money. The
action which follows includes Herne's falling in love, quarreling
with a friend, and establishing himself as a physician in Buenos
Aires under the pressures of a citywide epidemic. The sketch
suggests some real person among the young Englishmen whose
society Hudson cultivated in Buenos Aires after his father's
death.

Though in general *Ralph Herne* is a feeble piece of fiction—
the conversation stilted and the characters artificial—it is marked
by a few strokes which identify it with Hudson's more characteristic writings. There are references to flowers and to butter-
flies; and noting that the plague has killed the native sparrows
formerly so numerous, one of the characters remarks: "Buenos
Aires has lost its little orange-colored pet, and its shrill, merry
trills will probably be heard no more for some years. Probably
that sooty little ruffian, the London sparrow, would have lived
it out."[34]

The flyleaves of the Knopf edition of *Ralph Herne* as published in 1923 carry an almost indecipherable comment in Hudson's holograph, in which one sentence is fairly clear: "I have
never taken myself seriously . . . as a fictionist."[35]

CHAPTER 5

The Essayist About Birds

WITH two books published in successive years at the beginning of the present century, *Nature in Downland*
(1900) and *Birds and Man* (1901), Hudson attained his full maturity as a writer and established his position as one of the greatest
masters of the personal essay in any literature and of all time.
He reached the age of sixty in this period; and he began to reap
the fruits of the many small expeditions into the countryside
which had been a part of his life in England—whenever he
could find a few pounds to pay for them—and of all his extensive reading from his earliest years.

The foundation stuff—the raw material of these and the succeeding even greater books,—came from his expeditions: the
walking and cycling trips along country roads, the sojourns in
remote villages, the visits to forests and downlands and the sea-
coast. The texture of the essays was enriched by Hudson's constant reading and rereading and by the recurring juxtaposition
of the fresh experience of England with the richly and intensely
remembered experience of his earlier years in the Argentine.
In these general aspects, all of Hudson's work as an essayist, for
the remaining score of years of his life, was of one texture and
one character, varying only in emphasis upon specific subject
matter.

It was in the writing of these last years that Hudson attained
the full mastery in the matter of style which justifies the judgment of Ford Madox Ford and Joseph Conrad quoted in my
preface. The precise qualities of any writer's style are difficult
to pinpoint, though this is less true of some than of others. We
can recognize with a considerable degree of assurance certain
individualized and characteristic elements in the style of Thomas
Carlyle, of John Ruskin, of Walter Pater, of R. L. Stevenson, for

example; but those which mark Hudson's writing as his own lie deeper.

It is clear that what characterizes any writer's style as his own must rest ultimately on two factors: his choice of words and the patterns in which those words are arranged. The matter of diction is fairly simple; for, as Ford declared, the best writing is marked by the use of "fresh, usual words": words that arouse in the reader strong and clear response in the sensory imagination but words not so strong or so strange as to attract attention to themselves, thus diverting the reader from the total experience a given passage provides. In Hudson's essays, this test is triumphantly met. He gives us the most intimate, detailed, and precise experience of what he is describing or narrating without resorting to technical language or even to rare and unusual words which might send us to the dictionary.

But it is in the second basic factor in style that Hudson most excels—the factor, less easy to define, which I have called "the patterns in which words are arranged." These patterns are of three kinds. First, there are the grammatical patterns of phrases, clauses, and sentences. Here the primary marks of a good style are clarity and emphasis: the disposition of elements which most facilitates the reader's grasp of content without ambiguity or confusion; and the structuring of sentence and paragraph which results in reinforcement of the importance of major elements—in making what is most significant evidently so. These, the patterns of meaning, are essential in any style that is to achieve its purpose: they are as necessary in a textbook as in a personal essay.

But there are two other categories of "the patterns in which words are arranged": categories primarily exemplified in prose fiction and in the personal essay, though constantly present in all good prose—patterns of rhythm and patterns of sound. In *From Pampas to Hedgerows and Downs,* the most thorough and very sympathetic treatment which Hudson's writings have received, Richard E. Haymaker succeeds in exploring fruitfully the matter of rhythmical patterns in Hudson's prose. By an ingenious method of indicating stresses, he succeeds in showing how positive, rich, and varied are Hudson's prose rhythms. Even more diffused and elusive are the patterns of sound. Any good prose that has any degree of emotional content reveals these patterns, often as rich and as significant in effect as the sound patterns associated with poetry. For appreciation and full enjoyment of both patterns of rhythm and patterns of sound in Hudson's prose at its best, it is necessary to read it, or hear it read, aloud—a pleasure to which most careful readers of his work have testified. Maturity in these aspects of his writing Hudson reaches in these volumes of essays of his last two decades. His style is at once richer in rhythm and sound and more resourceful in vocabulary and in sentence structure than in his earlier work. At its amazingly frequent best in these volumes, it fully justifies the judgment of Ford and Conrad noted above.

There are eleven volumes of these later essays. These may be most fruitfully considered in three groups, distinguished by differences in subject matter, in emphasis, and in intention. Probably the most widely held knowledge of Hudson as an essayist is based on his writings about birds. Four books primarily about birds were published in this period of his life: *Birds in London* (1898), *Birds and Man* (1901), *Adventures Among Birds* (1913), and *Birds in Town and Village* (1919). We shall look at these first, in our review of Hudson's later work as an essayist. A second group consists of five books which deal primarily with specific portions of England, with broad treatment of the wild life of the given region (birds included but not dominant), and with great emphasis on human beings. This group of studies was initiated by *Nature in Downland* (1900), followed by *Hampshire Days* (1903), *The Land's End* (1908), and *Afoot in England* (1909), and culminated in *A Shepherd's Life* (1910). The third group includes the three volumes of essays published in the last three years of Hudson's life: *The Book of a Naturalist* (1919); *A Traveller in Little Things* (1921); and *A Hind in Richmond Park* (1922). These volumes are distinguished from those of the preceding groups by their wider range of subjects; by their individual expression of ideas, theories, speculations; and by their frequently argumentative tone. Any devoted reader of Hudson is bound to have favorites among these eleven books. We shall look at each volume individually, while recognizing its relationships with others in the series on grounds of subject matter, tone, and intention, rather than of chronological order.

II   Birds in London

Birds in London (1898) is actually more closely related to the "scientific" *British Birds,* also published in 1898, than to the more characteristic collections of essays on birds which followed it— *Adventures Among Birds* (1913) for example. The purpose of *Birds in London* is primarily propagandist: it indicts in particular collectors and, more pointedly, the general lack of public interest in, and knowledge of, birds. The book is therefore an expression of Hudson's advocacy of conservation, especially in relation to birds, which found its most vigorous expression in pamphlets he wrote at about the same time and also earlier in support of the Society for the Protection of Birds, founded in 1889.

The organization and method of *Birds in London* are in a measure scientific. The book essentially consists of a tour of London's parks, cemeteries, and other places in which birds may be observed; and the organization of the book is arranged in a geographical sequence circling the city. In each area, Hudson reports the birds to be seen; the care and protection given to the feathered residents, or the lack of these; and the possibilities for improvement in conditions and recommendations for steps in that direction. The book, addressed specifically to residents of London, is essentially an effort to arouse their interest in birds and to obtain their support for efforts to improve the conditions in which their birds have to live.

Though the book is rich in specific observations and incidents, which are recorded with Hudson's characteristic vividness and not infrequently with pungent pointedness, its nature and its purpose gave it much more appeal for the contemporary reader, particularly for Hudson's fellow residents of London, than it can have for the reader of seventy-odd years later, particularly one who has never visited London.

In spite of the many faults and failures in protection of and provision for birds which Hudson records in this book—often with vigorous indictment of those responsible—the prevailing tone of the work is positive and hopeful. Hudson believes that the people of London—even dwellers in the slums—enjoy birds and will in a great majority of cases support efforts for their protection and encouragement. He writes near the end of the book:

I know it is a common idea—one hears it often enough—that love of
birds is by no means a general feeling; that it is, on the contrary, somewhat rare, and consequently that those who experience it have some
reason to be proud of their superiority. To my mind all this is a pretty
delusion; no one flatters himself that he is in any special way a lover
of sunshine and green flowery meadows and running waters and shady
trees; and I can only repeat here what I have said before, that the
delight in a wild bird is as common to all men as the feeling that the
sunshine is sweet and pleasant to behold.[1]

III Birds and Man

In the first chapter of *Birds and Man* (1901) Hudson gives us
a clue to the attitude which marks all of his major essays. He
tells of a visit to a museum, in which he is repelled by the specimens of the rare and beautiful Dartford warbler displayed there:
"twisted by the stuffer into a variety of attitudes—ancient, dusty,
dead little birds, painful to look at—a libel on nature and an
insult to a man's intelligence." Yet Hudson observes that other
visitors to the museum are pleased by what they see: "I heard
many sincere expressions of admiration." He concludes:

they know no better. They have never properly seen anything in nature,
but have looked always with mind and the inner vision preoccupied
with other and familiar things—indoor scenes and objects, and scenes
described in books. If they had ever looked at wild birds properly—
that is to say, emotionally—the images of such sights would have remained in their minds: and, with such a standard for comparison, these
dreary remnants of dead things set before them as restorations and as
semblances of life would have only produced a profundly depressing
effect.[2]

By "emotionally," as Hudson uses the word here, I think he
means two things. It means *intensely,* with active attentiveness,
so that details of color and action, of sound and setting, are
registered precisely in the consciousness of the observer: not
blurred or vague but sharp and definite as items of specific experience. Thus far the requirement is that applicable to the
scientific observer, the ornithologist for whom accuracy is essential. But for Hudson, "emotionally" also means *with insight,* with
a degree of participation in the life of the creatures observed,
with understanding, even with empathy. To the Hudson of the

great essays, nature is something beyond external observation, however accurate; it demands participation, vicarious experience, the will and power to enter into and be a part of, however imperfectly, the life observed. This quality in Hudson, pervading all his characteristic writing, sets him apart from, and above, most writers about nature.

This quality is not sentimentalism, for it is untainted by falsity. Real and intense, it embraces the dangers, the fatigue and distress and disaster, the ultimate death, of all living things. This wholeness of vision, which not merely sees the creature at the moment but includes in its perception the whole range of experience for any living thing, is the mark of Hudson's greatness. It is expressed sometimes lightly, playfully, and in minor matters, as in his comment on Herbert Spencer's view:

Speaking of the mental processes of the cow, he tells us just how that large mammal is impressed by the sight of birds that come near it and pass across its field of vision: they are regarded in a vague way, as mere shadows, or shadowy objects, flitting or blown about hither and thither over the grass or through the air. He didn't know a cow's mind. My conviction is that all animals distinctly see in those of other species, living, sentient, intelligent beings like themselves; and that, when birds and mammals meet together, they take pleasure in the consciousness of one another's presence, in spite of the enormous difference in size, voice, habits, etc.[3]

At a far deeper level, in the essay on "Owls in a Village" in *Birds and Man,* Hudson asks whether the hooting of the owl has the same meaning for us that it had for Paleolithic man,

the human being that did not walk erect, and smile, and look on heaven, but went with a stoop, looking on the earth? No, and Yes. Standing alone under the great trees in the dark still nights, the sound seems to increase the feeling of loneliness, to make the gloom deeper, the silence more profound. Turning our vision inward on such occasions, we are startled with a glimpse of the night-side of nature in the soul. . . .[4]

Hudson's vision of earth is never lacking in this perception of the "night-side" of life. In the same chapter, sharing with his reader his experience in looking across a wide expanse of coun-

try in which he sees "the idle hedges enclosing vacant fields"⁵—
where the farms have been abandoned and the villages deserted—
he is visited by "a vision of a time to come and of an England
dispeopled."⁶

I have suggested that this wholeness of vision, embracing all
the facts, black as well as bright, is one of the basic elements in
Hudson's greatness as a writer. The other is, of course, his style,
which comes to full flowering in these books which mark his
full maturity and which confronts the reader immediately with
the mystery which marks its indisputable excellence. Indeed, the
style of W. H. Hudson defies ultimate analysis or complete objective statement of the sources of its beauty and its power. We
can recognize certain things about it. We can see that it is consistently concrete—that it achieves a constantly rich flow of
specific imaginative experience for the reader through its choice
of words, without the slightest suggestion of strained search for
the best. We can see that it is notably rhythmical, the patterns
of words both in rhythm and sound richly contributory to the
total impression intended without ever exhibiting effort or manip-
ulation. But beyond these fairly obvious general observations, it
is hard to go. Hudson's style never obtrudes itself upon the
reader's consciousness; it never demands attention to itself. Yet
it never fails the reader, never falls short of a rich and full and
memorable sharing of experience. Occasionally, as the material
demands, it quickens and tightens in an imperative eloquence.
Such a passage is that in the essay, "Early Spring in Savernake
Forest," in which Hudson shares with us his experience of listening to the wind:

That is a mysterious voice which the forest has: it speaks to us, and
somehow the life it expresses seems nearer, more intimate, than that
of the sea. Doubtless because we are ourselves terrestrial and woodland
in our origin; also because the sound is infinitely more varied as well
as more human in character. There are sighings and moanings, and
wails and shrieks, and wind-blown murmurings, like the distant confused talking of a vast multitude. A high wind in an extensive wood
always produces this effect of numbers.⁷

In succeeding sentences Hudson amplifies this comparison of the
sound of a gentle wind to that "of a vast concourse—crowds and
congregations, tumultuous or orderly, but all swayed by one

absorbing impulse, solemn or passionate": "Through the near whisperings a deeper, louder sound comes from a distance. It rumbles like thunder, falling and rising as it rolls onwards; it is antiphonal, but changes as it travels nearer. Then there is no longer demand and response; the smitten trees are all bent one way, and their innumerable voices are as one voice, expressing we know not what, but always something not wholly strange to us—lament, entreaty, denunciation."[8]

Almost immediately following this remarkable passage, in which the appeal is primarily to the sense of hearing, is another paragraph in which visual imagery is primary. It is a passage devoted to sharing Hudson's experience of beech leaves. "It is a leaf that refuses to die wholly," he tells us:

the beech leaf keeps its sharp clean edges unbroken, its hard texture and fiery colour, its buoyancy and rustling incisive hollows and beaten down by rains, the leaves lie mingled in one dead, sodden mass for days and weeks at a time, and appear ready to mix with the soil; but frost and sun suck up the moisture and the dead come to life again. They glow like fire, and tremble at every breath. It was strange and beautiful to see them lying all around me, glowing copper and red and gold when the sun was strong on them, not dead, but sleeping like a bright-coloured serpent in the genial warmth; to see, when the wind found them, how they trembled, and moved as if awakening; and as the breath increased rose up in twos and threes and half-dozens here and there, chasing one another a little way, hissing and rustling; then all at once, struck by a violent gust, they would be up in thousands, eddying round and round in a dance, and, whirling aloft, scatter and float among the lofty branches to which they were once attached.[9]

In the same chapter from which these passages are quoted, we find an interesting example of Hudson's not infrequent, mildly sarcastic rebukes of "closet" naturalists who base their accounts of living things on "authorities" rather than on their own observation. He tells us that he had been condemned by "a distinguished naturalist, who reviewed the book in one of the papers," for his statement in *British Birds* that jays congregate in flocks in the spring before nesting time. Hudson notes that he knows exactly where that naturalist's "knowledge of the habits of the jay was derived"—from "a book published ninety-nine

years ago."[10] Hudson proceeds to discuss the varying vocal utter-
ances of jays, asserting that the jay does have a real song but
that it is "something of a puzzle, as it is not the same song in
any two places"; and he gives us the idea that there is no inherited and no traditional song for this species but that "each
bird that has a song has invented it for himself."[11]

In further expression of Hudson's characteristic extreme interest in the songs of birds, *Birds and Man* contains at the end
of a chapter called "The Secret of the Willow Wren" a detailed
analysis of the relation of bird music to music of human composition or utterance, and of the basis of the varying appeal of
the music of different birds. His conclusion is "that the various
sensations excited in us by the cries, moans, screams and the
more or less musical notes of various species, are due to the human emotions which they express or seem to express."[12]

One of the elements in *Birds and Man* which identify this
work as that of the mature Hudson is the incidence in it of
emphasis on human beings and experience—the aspect which
Hudson no doubt wished to suggest by the title *Birds and Man.*
Scarcely a chapter of the fifteen which constitute the volume
but contains a human person, sharply etched and warmly memorable even if only briefly presented. Some of these characterizations are rather sharply critical: the "pale young curate" whose
reading of the Service is a mere gabble; the "big repulsive looking man in a black greasy coat—a human animal to be avoided—"
who confides to Hudson his expectation of shortly doing "something very good indeed" in the matter of Dartford warblers. He
is a collector of bird skins for wealthy buyers who want mounted
specimens, and he has come to the region where this nearly
extinct species may still be found. In contrast is Hudson's sympathetic treatment of a farm laborer who recounts experiences
which seem to indicate that the hooting of owls in daylight is an
omen of death.

A final evidence of the maturity of Hudson's writing in *Birds
and Man* is the increased range and thoughtfulness of the reading reflected in it. Before *Birds and Man* appeared, he had come
to know personally several contemporary writers, and he had
been recognized by a few for the great writer he was. That
recognition was widening rapidly during the period in which
he wrote *Birds and Man.* He quotes W. B. Yeats, and he men-

tions correspondence with W. E. Henley, who "took me to task on account of some jeering remarks made about our poets' way of treating the birds. . . ."[13] There are favorable references to his fellow naturalist John Burroughs; and the last chapter of the book, "Selborne," is devoted to Hudson's most extended tribute to another writer in the whole range of his work: to Gilbert White, in the concrete terms of Hudson's experience in visiting the village about which White had written.

IV Adventures among Birds

Adventures among Birds (1913) follows essentially the lines laid down in Hudson's earlier volume, *Birds and Man*. It brings together some twenty brief essays, some of which had been published in periodicals but were "altered and extended," as Hudson tells us in a prefatory note, for this volume. As always in Hudson's essays, the material is fundamentally that of his own experience: his observations are recorded at various times and places, including in this book several differing areas of England, amplified and illuminated by his reflections and his reading.

The material of this collection, in spite of its title, is less clearly focused on birds alone than is that of *Birds and Man*. One of the most interesting chapters to the general reader is that on "Friendship in Animals." Hudson holds that a capacity for genuine friendship, exceeding and differing from general group loyalty and from definite self-interest, exists among animals. This well-organized chapter contains a dozen specific instances of what Hudson calls friendship between animals, including birds, and between animals and human beings. Hudson begins with recollection of the unmistakable friendships among horses, the clear preference for association with a single individual, which he had observed as a boy in the Argentine. He then gives several astonishing (but fully authenticated) examples of the recognition of a human friend by a bird or animal after a long separation and of the helpfulness of birds and other animals to crippled members of their own species.

One of the best chapters in this or indeed in any of Hudson's collections is the brief "In a Hampshire Village." It is devoted entirely to portrayal of human beings: the young workman and his wife with whom Hudson lived for a time and their only child, a boy. He admires their thrift, their gentleness of manner, and their obvious deep devotion to each other. Only at the end of his stay does the young wife and mother confide to him their secret grief—the sudden death, from a disease mistakenly treated, of a younger child nearly two years before—a very beautiful little girl and distinguished by an extreme love of flowers and of all living things. The loss had caused them to move to the village from the heath where they had lived before but which had now become unendurable because of the loss of the child who had loved it so much. The story of this revelation is told by Hudson so simply and quietly and understandingly that it is profoundly moving to the reader.

V Birds in Town and Village

In some ways *Birds in Town and Village* (1919) is one of the most interesting collections of essays about birds because it contains the earliest and most of the latest of Hudson's writing about British birds. In 1893 he issued a volume entitled *Birds in a Village,* which has never been reprinted in its original form. In a brief preface to *Birds in Town and Village,* dated September, 1919, he tells us that, for this later volume, the earlier one has been "mostly rewritten with some fresh matter added, mainly later observations and incidents introduced in illustration of the various subjects discussed. For the concluding portion of the old book, which has been discarded, I have substituted entirely new matter—the part entitled 'Birds in a Cornish Village.'"

Between the revised earlier portion and the "new matter," Hudson presents in the volume of 1919 five essays "which I have retained with little alteration." These include the vehement and bitter attack, in the essay "Exotic Birds for Britain," on "the feather-wearing fashion" and on "the London trade in dead birds and the refusal of women at that time to help us in trying to save the beautiful wild bird life of this country and of the world generally from extermination." Hudson, who finds reason in 1919 to congratulate himself and the nation for a profound change in attitude in these matters, gives credit especially to the Royal Society for the Protection of Birds.

In the third essay from the earlier volume which Hudson used in *Birds in Town and Village,* we find a striking example of the kind of writing through which Hudson achieved effectiveness as an advocate of a more civilized and enlightened attitude toward birds and as a protester against their senseless destruction. He tells of a young man who proudly showed three stuffed king-fishers in a case, "and informed me that he had shot them at a place (which he named) quite close to London. He said that these three birds were the last of their kind ever seen there; that he had gone, week after week and watched and waited, until one by one, at long intervals he had secured them all; and that two years had passed since the last one was killed, and no other kingfisher had been seen at the place."

Hudson comments that the place mentioned was one fre-quented "by crowds of London working people" on weekends and holidays and that "hundreds, perhaps thousands, of pairs of tired eyes would have been freshened and gladdened by the sight of their gem-like beauty." But this knowledge only made the young man "prouder of his achievement." Hudson excuses the young man, on the ground that he was "a cockney of the small shop-keeping class—a Philistine of the Philistines."[14] But he proceeds to turn the full force of his indictment on "that writer whose masterly works on English rural life are familiar to everyone," who "relates that he invariably carried a gun when out of doors, mainly with the object of shooting any kingfisher he might chance to see" because "the dead bird always formed an acceptable present to the cottager's wife, who would get it stuffed and keep it as an ornament on her parlour mantelshelf!"[15] Hudson does not mention the name of the eminent author, but he identifies him sufficiently lower on the page as the author of *Wild Life in a Southern Country*—Richard Jefferies. Hudson was no respecter of persons in his campaign against meaningless slaughter of birds, as this and many other passages attest.

The village of *Birds in a Village* is not specifically identified, but Hudson tells us it was "not more than twenty-five minutes' walk from a small station" which he could reach in less than one hour by rail from London. The essays of this first volume about birds were products of many brief visits to this village, before Hudson had fully established his habit of spending longer periods in the countryside and of traveling greater distances.

The characteristic methods and lines of emphasis illustrated in the later books are already present in the volume of 1893, at least as Hudson rewrote it for publication in 1919. One of these is the attention to specific human beings and groups of human beings which serves to keep the writings about birds and nature in general in these volumes in a human perspective. This quality is amusingly illustrated in the second essay. Hudson is at the moment especially interested in badgers, wishing to observe them and to learn more of their habits. Thinking the area around the village a promising one for observation of these animals, he questions a group of men at the local tap about badgers. He is greeted with a dead silence, a positive withdrawal from conversation, and a refusal to answer his questions—all of which puzzles him. Too late he learns that in other villages nearby and in the countryside the residents of his chosen village are referred to as "badgers," as a term of derogation in reference to their character and habits. But he writes that "it was not remembered against me that I had wounded their sensibilities; they soon found out that I was nothing but a harmless field naturalist, and I had friendly relations with many of them."[16]

In the essay "Moorhens in Hyde Park" Hudson rejoices in the annual return of migrating birds to London. He does not understand why they come, since it would seem more natural "for them to keep aloof from our dimmed atmosphere, and the rude sounds of traffic, and the sight of many people going to and fro." But come they do, "and all London is ringed around with a mist of melody, which presses on us, ambitious of winning its way even to the central heart of our citadel, creeping in, mistlike, along gardens and tree-planted roads, clinging to the greenery of parks and squares, and floating above the dull noises of the town as clouds fleecy and ethereal float above the earth."[17]

Watching four canaries in a cage (not his own), Hudson quotes Matthew Arnold's "feeling lines on his dead canary, 'Poor Matthias!'" He comments that Arnold is a poet, "and the author of much good verse, which I appreciate and hold dear. But he was not a naturalist. . . ." Hudson holds that "the wishes, thronging the restless little feathered breast" are not altogether so incommunicable as the melodious mourner of "Poor Matthias" imagines. "The days—ay, and years—which I have spent in the society of my feathered friends have not, I flatter myself, been so wasted that I cannot small my soul, just as the preacher smalled his voice, to bring it within reach of them, and establish some sort of passage."[18] This passage is one of the extremely infrequent ones in Hudson's writing in which he makes a claim, even a modest one, for his own right to speak with authority.

Another of these rare instances occurs in Chapter 10 of *Birds in a Village* in Hudson's account of a hedge-sparrow laboring furiously to supply the appetite of a young cuckoo: the product of an egg laid in her nest by its parasitical parent, probably to the destruction for her own young. Hudson comments: "I can safely say, I think, that no man has observed so many parasitical young birds (individuals) being fed by their foster-parents as myself, yet the interest such a sight inspired in me is just as fresh now as in boyhood."[19] The reference is to the study of the parasitical cowbirds of Argentina that Hudson undertook in his boyhood and youth, which resulted in important discoveries about them.

In an additional comment about the caged canaries mentioned above in connection with Arnold's poem, Hudson professes to quote one of them after putting some leaves in the cage: "*I tasted them out of compliment to nature, though they were scarcely palatable. . . .*" Then he comments, "No, that was not my own expression; it was said by Thoreau, perhaps the only human a little bird can quote with approval."[20] In the preceding essay, there also is a reference to Thoreau—"that 'finer way' which Thoreau found and put aside his fowling-piece to practice";[21] and in a third essay of this group, "Chanticleer," in which Hudson is discussing the crowing of the cock as a prelude to morning, he again mentions the American:

I thought that it might be worth while keeping a cockerel for his music merely, as a singing bird. The note of this once wild Indian pheasant is certainly the most remarkable of any bird's, and if they could be naturalized without being domesticated it would soon become the most famous sound in our woods. . . . To walk in a winter morning in a wood where these birds abounded, their native woods, and hear the wild cockerels crow on the trees, clear and shrill for miles over the surrounding country—think of it! It would put nations on the alert. Who would not be early to rise, and rise earlier and earlier on each successive morning of his life, till he became unspeakably healthy, wealthy, and wise?[22]

After this comment on Thoreau's praise of cockerels, Hudson then speaks of "one in some ways greater than Thoreau, so unlike the skyey-minded New England prophet and solitary, so much more genial and tolerant, more mundane and lovable; and yet like Thoreau in his nearness to nature." Hudson is referring to Chaucer, and he proceeds to praise "that wonderful tale of the 'Nun's Priest,' in which the whole character of Chanticleer, his glory and his foibles, together with the homely virtues of Dame Partlett, are so admirably set forth."[23]

A few pages earlier Hudson has indulged in vigorous criticism of Milton—of what he calls "the one bad couplet in L'Allegro": "While the cock with lively din scatters the rear of darkness thin." Hudson, who objects vigorously to "lively din," asserts that the only picture the phrase gives him is "of a stalwart, bare-armed, blowsy-faced woman, vigorously beating on a tin pan with a stick; but for what purpose—whether to call down a passing swarm of bees, or to summon the chickens to be fed—I never know": The second line, he says, gives only confused impressions—"a chaos utterly unlike the serenity and imperceptible growth of morning, and not a picture at all."[24]

Hudson's humor, usually quiet and restrained though always pointed, becomes vigorous in the final essay of this group, "In an Old Garden," when he describes the irruption of "those three demoniacal fox-terriers, Snap, Puzzy, and Babs," belonging to his hostess, who frighten away the birds he has been watching. But they lead him to a reflection which affords a memorable ending to this beautiful essay, and also suggests the wider range of speculation which we find in his final work in this form: "It is a consolation to think that they are not my pets; that I shall not grieve, like their mistress, when their brief barking period is over; that I care just so much and no more for them than for any other living creature. . . . None are out of place where Nature placed them, nor unbeautiful; none are unlovable. . . ."[25]

CHAPTER 6

Books About Places and People

IN the last ten years of his work as a writer, W. H. Hudson achieved his full maturity and his highest distinction. The focus of his work gradually shifted from the direct observation of birds and the life of earth to human beings and their experience of that life. Increasingly, his later books are about people; and he goes in his final writings beyond the specific recording of their experience to analysis of its significance and ultimate meaning and value.

With *Nature in Downland* (1900), Hudson initiated both the new century and the series of eleven volumes of great personal essays which constitute his clearest claim to recognition as a writer of the first rank. As I have suggested before, these eleven books fall into three fairly definite groups because of their subject matter: (1) those which deal primarily with birds and record at once Hudson's observations and his beliefs, emotions, and reflections concerning birds; (2) those which have a broader reach and in general a deeper meaning because of their emphasis on human beings and their lives in relation to the earth; and (3) books essentially or ultimately reflective and interpretative in purpose, though rich in the elements of direct observation and in concrete rendering of experience.

Nature in Downland is the first and one of the finest of the volumes which constitute the second group. It was followed by four others of similar character: *Hampshire Days* (1903); *The Land's End* (1908); *Afoot in England* (1909) and— the culmination of the series and, in the judgment of some of Hudson's most appreciative readers, his highest individual achievement—*A Shepherd's Life* (1910).

Nature in Downland sets the pattern for the four volumes just mentioned which were to follow it. In each Hudson makes choice of a specific area of the British countryside which he had come to know well through many expeditions, walking or cycling, and through brief periods of sustained residence at different seasons of the year. Hudson shares with his reader the essence of his actual experience of the region in terms of his observation and interpretation of all aspects of it: the nature of the landscape as a whole; the conditioning weather and climate; and all forms of animate life which this part of the British earth sustains—plants, insects, animals—including birds and human beings.

The books produced under these circumstances and with this intention realize for the receptive reader a fuller experience of a region than most of us ever attain in a lifetime of residence in a specific place. No method of summary and sampling can do justice to Hudson's achievement, nor can it do more than suggest the richness and integrity of the vicarious experience which these books offer to the reader.

I Nature in Downland

Nature in Downland affords at the outset immediate immersion in strongly realized personal experience. Hudson takes us with him to spend "a good many hours on the top of Kingston Hill." With him, we view the prospect from "the flat top of that very long hill . . . the sea of downland and the grey glinting ocean beyond on one side, the immense expanse of the wooded Sussex weald on the other," all partially covered "with a blue obscuring haze." We feel the violence of the wind on this height; then, immediately we look closely and long through Hudson's eyes at the abundant blowing thistledown; and with him we give ourselves up "to the pleasure of it, wishing for no better thing."[1]

This down leads to Hudson's vivid recollection of his boyhood on the pampas, when the watching of blowing thistledown was a frequent and fascinating experience. The Argentinian thistledown was much "larger and whiter and infinitely more abundant," he tells us. "After a day or days of wind it would be found in immense masses in the sheltered hollows, or among the tall standing stalks of the dry plants";[2] and he and his brothers liked to gallop their horses through these drifts, to the terror of the horses.

Hudson now turns to the "smaller, more fragile English thistledown" and discovers that its beauty is accentuated by its color: "Seen against the deep greens and browns of the vegetation in late summer it appears white, but compared with a white feather or white flower we see that it is silvery, with a faint yellow or brown tinge, lighter but a little like the brown tinge in the glistening transparent wings of some dragon-flies and other insects."[3] This precision and vividness in rendering details in nature are two of Hudson's most characteristic qualities, illustrated on almost every page of these books of essays.

Before we get far into this first chapter of Hudson's first fully characteristic book of essays, we find a second individualizing method and quality which we shall encounter again and again in our consideration of them: his way of supplementing and illuminating his subject from his wide resources of reading. True, he declares in this chapter that "I am not a great reader, and know few books, that on this subject I therefore speak as a fool, or, at all events, an ignorant person."[4] But this self-indictment can be dismissed as highly exaggerated—as true only in the sense that Hudson is not a "bookish" person and that his actual experience of life and things through his own senses is more important to him than all that books can give. Actually, he was a constant and perceptive reader; in range of interest and response, he was a far better reader of literature both old and new than most of his contemporaries, including the most learned and scholarly among them. The page on which the disclaimer appears happens to face one on which "old Ben Jonson" is quoted; and it is preceded and followed by passages about books and writers which would make Nature in Downland primarily a book of literary criticism if they and others like them were its most characteristic element.

One of these passages also involved an echo of Argentina. As a boy, in a period of sustained ill health which prevented his indulgence in his preferred outdoor activities (as mentioned in a preceding chapter), Hudson read voraciously in the extensive library—largely of eighteenth- and early nineteenth-century writers—collected by his parents. Among the writings he enjoyed so much that he was able to quote a description of a bird's nest from it from memory some fifty years later was Reverend James Hurdis' Village Curate. Hudson tells us that his admiration for this passage rose from his own extreme admiration for and wonder at the exquisite craftsmanship displayed by some kinds of birds in the making of their nests:

For though so admirably fashioned—whether attached to slender swaying reeds and rushes, or placed down among the grasses, or on wood, or high among the clustering leaves on trees—as to seem a natural growth, with their gem-like pearly and speckled eggs, many-coloured, resting in them like bright polished seeds in an opening capsule, yet it was not so; they had not been produced by Nature like leaf and flower and fruit, but were artificial basket-houses built with much labour, with many selected materials gathered in many places, by the little winged men and women called birds.[5]

Hudson then tells us how he has recently acquired a book of Hurdis' poetry, and he is "compelled to say that it is very bad poetry, reminding one, in its prosy diction and occasional rhetorical outbursts, now of *The Task* and now of *The Seasons*."[6] Yet in ,Hurdis' memory Hudson went the following Sunday to what had been Hurdis' church at the village of Bishopstone—where we encounter with him a concrete experience representative of those that mark this and all his succeeding books about rural England:

I was so fortunate as to have a seat near the middle of the church, abreast of the side door which stood wide open admitting the summer light and warmth and outdoor sounds; so that while following the service I could let my eyes rest on the landscape. That was a beautiful picture I had to look at, with the doorway for frame; a round yellow hill and the blue sky beyond, and between the hill and the church a green meadow, low outhouse and fences, and a small paddock or enclosure with rooks and daws and small birds coming and going. And by-and-by, into that green enclosure came a white calf, and remained there for some time, standing motionless, in the centre of the picture. The brilliant sunlight made it luminous, and it was like a calf hewn out of a block of purest white chalk.[7]

Though James Hurdis, no more than other writers, had done justice to the downland country in literature, Hudson expresses belief—still in this first chapter—that Richard Jefferies might have done so had he lived long enough after making this region his home. His comment about Jefferies is perhaps the longest and most frankly personal in his work; he had profound admiration for his ability and sympathy for his sufferings. The reference to Jefferies is continued to tell us that Hudson is "writing this introductory chapter in the last house he inhabited, and where

he died." It was a custom of Hudson's, in the expeditions from
London in which he found the materials for his books of essays,
to visit and if possible to live in places which held for him significant literary associations.

I have considered the first chapter of *Nature in Downland* in
some detail because it illustrates so brilliantly the characteristic
methods and effects of Hudson's writing in all the books of
essays which follow. Chapter titles—"The Shepherd of the
Downs," "Silence and Music," and a dozen more—indicate the
rich completeness of this evocation and expression of a region.
The sureness and resourcefulness with which Hudson summons
literary allusion and quotation to his use seem to me especially
remarkable in this book. Following a passage in which Hudson
vividly describes the black oxen which he sees used for plowing
in Downland, he speculates as to whether similar draft animals
are used in Ireland, commenting: "At all events, it seems unlikely
that a Nationalist and leader of the Celtic school, Mr. W. B.
Yeats, should have come to the most Saxon district in England
to get that grand and sombre simile with which he concludes
his poetic drama of *The Countess Cathleen:*

> Tell them that walk upon the floor of peace
> That I would die and go to her I love;
> The years like great black oxen tread the world.
> And God the herdsman goads them on behind,
> And I am broken by their passing feet.[8]

A more surprising glimpse of the range of Hudson's reading is
found in the chapter "Summer Heat." In his rambles Hudson
comes upon a group of five farm children "lying on the grass on
the slope of a down,"

The sight of their happiness brought back to contrast "the
vision of old Piers Plowman, ill-fed and gaunt and ragged, following his plough on a winter's day—the picture which has often
made me shiver with the sensation of remembered cold. Lines
that had printed themselves indelibly on my memory, so keenly
did I feel them when I read them, now seemed all at once to
have a new and deeper significance." He proceeds to quote
sixteen lines of Langland's vision and to comment about Langland's firm conviction that, as surely as summer follows winter,

"for poor humanity there is a glorious eternal summer after this life's bitter winter."[9]

Among other writers quoted or mentioned by Hudson in *Nature in Downland* are John Gerarde of the famous *Herbal*, Milton, Sterne, Cowper, Keats, De Quincey, Charles Lamb, Tennyson, F. W. H. Myers, and his admired Gilbert White.

One of the most charming chapters of the book—charming in a rather precise sense—is that entitled "A Fairy Fauna" which deals with the small creatures of the downs: snails, flies, butter-flies, bees, and others. Of the butterflies of the downs, he notes that "Most abundant is the little pale blue of the chalk downs; in fact, he outnumbers all the others together. Sitting on the grass, you can sometimes count as many as thirty or forty flut-tering about in sight and near you at one time."[10] At the end of the chapter Hudson speaks of De Quincey as having written "very prettily about what he called 'gluttonism'—the craving of the mind to know and enjoy all the good literature and music and art-work that had been produced; and finally to know the lives of all men—all who are living and all who had lived on the earth."[11] Hudson deprecates this wish, declaring:

if the power to attain to all that De Quincey craved, or pretended that he craved for, were mine, I should not value it; I should give it all to be able to transform myself for the space of a summer's day into one of these little creatures on the South Downs; then to return to my own form and place in nature with a clear recollection of the wonderland in which I had been.[12]

He would give very careful consideration, Hudson says, to his choice of an insect, "since they differ as greatly from each other as bird from serpent, and fish from mammal. I should pass in review the slow beetle, heavily armoured, and the fantastic fly, a miracle of inconsequence; the esteemed humble-bee, and the wasp, that very fine insect gentleman in his mood of devilish cheerfulness,"[13] and many others. "And after all, I should make choice of the little blue butterfly, despite his smallness and fri-volity, to house myself in. The knowledge of that strange fairy world it inhabits would be incommunicable, like the vision vouchsafed to some religionist of which he has been forbidden to speak; but the memory of it would be a secret perennial joy."[14]

But the greatest richness of *Nature in Downland* is in the human beings who appear in and move through its pages, who speak and are known. No less than twenty people of the downlands we meet in its pages, varied and vivid, firmly individualized, persons. There are workmen, especially shepherds, folk of the quality of the old carter met by the shore in the first chapter—a group from which Hudson was to draw the great central character of *A Shepherd's Life;* a man just out of jail; a landlady and her husband who have become members of the Salvation Army and are happily preparing a pet lamb to be shown in an army parade; a man who knows the habits of swifts; a landlady who tells the story of a magpie which stole a sovereign, all the money in the house for purchase of a week's food; a woman in Chichester who tells Hudson how the calves brought to market for sale and slaughter in the town of Chichester used to break her heart with their bawling. The chapter on Chichester is in sharpest contrast to all the other content of the volume. Hudson found Chichester dirty physically and depraved morally—a hateful place. His vigorous indictment of "city" as encountered here serves as a sharp contrast to the sense of soundness and beauty and worth in life which is maintained in the other chapters of the book.

II   Hampshire Days

Hampshire Days (1903), one of the richest of Hudson's books in the group of those devoted to studies of specific areas of England, is rich in style and in substance, in the fully conveyed vivid experience of woods and fields, of birds and other animals, of trees and flowers, and of human beings. Indeed, it is equaled or surpassed in quality only by the later book dealing with the same region, *A Shepherd's Life.*

Early in the pages of *Hampshire Days* the reader encounters one of Hudson's characteristic passages of reflection—one on the subject of pain. It begins with an account of the ejection of a baby robin from its nest by a young cuckoo, that has been hatched from an egg deposited in the nest by the parasitical bird. The helpless, featherless baby robin has not fallen to the ground and thus quickly perished; it remains on a leaf only a few inches from the nest and in full sight of the mother robin. But it is too young to have a voice, and she pays no attention to it—

she is busy feeding and warming the infant cuckoo. The baby robin is doomed to die quickly of cold and starvation.

Hudson argues that the baby robin does not feel what we call "pain." The bird is nearly like a chick in the shell: it may have a glimmer of consciousness, but it is not able actually to feel pain. He is far from denying the reality and universality of pain, however:

the fact that as things are designed in this world of sentient life there can be no good, no sweetness or pleasure in life, nor peace and contentment and safety, nor happiness and joy, nor any beauty or strength or lustre, nor any bright and shining quality of body or mind, without pain, which is not an accident, nor an incident, nor something ancillary to life, but is involved in and a part of life, of its very colour and texture.[15]

One of the most arresting passages in *Hampshire Days* is one in which Hudson tells of witnessing, alone on the heath near nightfall, the killing of one flying insect by another: "They were locked together, and I saw the attacking insect raise his head and the forepart of his body so as to strike, then plunge his rostrum like a dagger in the soft part of his victim's body. Again and again he raised and buried his weapon in the other, and the other still refused to die or to cease struggling." The feeling of "intense repugnance" which the sight aroused in him was due, Hudson tells us, wholly to association; he had seen (in his boyhood in the Argentine) "just such a combat between two men, one fallen and the other on him, raising and striking down with his knife."[16]

Hudson lingers, thinking, while the darkness comes over the heath. He realizes then that he is near the "Pixie mounds, the barrows raised by probably prehistoric men, a people inconceivably remote in time and spirit from us."[17] The ensuing reflective passage, too long for quotation in its entirety, is one of the most memorable in all of Hudson's writing. It begins with his realization that he feels nearer in spirit to these ancient men, builders of the barrows, than to his contemporaries: "There are times and moods in which it is revealed to us, or to a few amongst us, that we are a survival of the past, a dying remnant of a vanished people, and are like strangers and captives among those who do not understand us, and have no wish to do so; whose language and customs and thoughts are not ours."[18] He rejects the suggestion that he is speaking of what some contemporary poets—William Watson and others—call "world-strangeness." He is expressing instead his sense of kinship with sky and soil, with wind and rain and sunshine, and his alienation from the life of cities—the "artificial life" which he so vigorously condemns and rejects.

This passage leads into a vision in which, sitting on one of the ancient barrows in the night, Hudson feels himself surrounded in the darkness by those people of ancient times—all looking with fear and hate toward the towns not far away . . . by which they and their way of life are threatened. "But they do not resent my presence, and would not resent it were I permitted to come at last to dwell with them for ever. Perhaps they know me for one of their tribe—know that what they feel I feel, would hate what they hate." "Love itself is an argument for immortality," Hudson says, seemingly with acceptance. "But love without hate I do not know and cannot conceive; one implies the other. No good and no bad quality or principle can exist (for me) without its opposite." He ends the passage by quoting Langland: "For by luthere men know the good; / And whereby wiste men which were white / If all things black were?"[19]

Hudson's inveterate dislike of collectors, who kill things for the sake of possessing their dead forms, appears vigorously in an account—partially humorous but essentially serious—of a conversation with a clergyman who announces that he is a lepidopterist. When Hudson tells him of the delight he has experienced in watching a hummingbird moth "suspended on his misty wings among the tall flowers in the August sunshine," which has seemed to him "one of the most beautiful things in nature,"[20] the lepidopterist-clergyman remarks that it has been a poor year for hummingbirds (using, of course, the scientific name, as Hudson has not). He has seen but three, and the first two he was able to capture easily, since he had his net with him. The third came fluttering above the flowers in a garden where he was visiting an old lady, one of his parishioners. Not having his net, he watched the moth while continuing his conversation until it fluttered near

him, and then he captured it with a swift grasp of the hand—
startling the old lady. Hudson comments acidly:

This same lepidopterist may be dead now, although a couple of summers ago he looked remarkably well and in the prime of life; but I
see that someone else is now parson of his parish. I have not taken
the pains to inquire; but, dead or alive, I cannot imagine him, in that
beautiful country of the Future which he perhaps spoke about to the
old cottage woman—I cannot imagine him in white raiment, with a
golden harp in his hand; for if here, in this country, he could see
nothing in a humming-bird hawk-moth among the flowers in the
sunshine but an object to be collected, what in the name of wonder
will he have to harp about![21]

The human portrait with which Hudson ends *Hampshire Days*
(except for a few notes on the departure of the swallows) is
one of the most vivid and memorable of the many his books
provide. It is an account of an old cottage woman, one of "an
old married couple, hard workers still with spade and hoe, and
able to make a living by selling the produce of their garden."[22]
This sketch, in contrast to most of Hudson's detailed presentation of human characters, is in dialogue—more precisely, mono-
logue—in which the old woman reveals herself and illuminates
her life. The outpouring is prompted by Hudson's question as to
what she is going to do with the fruit of a group of old elder
trees growing close to the cottage, "their branches bent and
hanging with the weight of the purpling clusters."[23]
"Do!" she exclaimed rather fiercely. "I'm going to do nothing
with it." Elderberry wine has been to her a familiar drink from
childhood: "And very good it were, too, I tell'e, in cold weather
in winter, made hot. It warmed your inside." But now nobody
wants it: "Nothing's good enough now unless you buys it in a
public-house or a shop." For two pages the old woman rants on,
her discourse reported by Hudson with just enough of her dialect
to give it flavor without becoming a distraction or an obstacle.
We see her standing in her crowded and cluttered garden, with
Hudson's tall angular form, head bent down to listen, and hear
her shrill querulous voice; and one shares with Hudson his
surprise at the ending of her diatribe, with its sudden softening:

People say to me, "Oh, don't talk to me about they blackbirds—they be

the worst of all for fruit." But I never minded that—because—well, I'tell
'e. I mind when I were a little thing at old Alresford, where I were
born, I used to be up at four in the morning, in summer, listening to
the blackbirds. And mother she used to say, "Lord, how she do love
to hear a blackbird!" It's always been the same. I'm always up at four,
and in summer I goes out to hear the blackbird when it do sing so
beautiful. But them starlings that come messing about, pulling the
straw out of the thatch, I've no patience with they. We didn't have
so many starlings when I were young. But things is very different
now; and what I say is, I wish they wasn't—I wish they was the same
as when I were a girl. And I wish I was a girl again."[24]

Hudson comments that "her wish, strange in these weary days,
to have her hard life to live over again, came as a surprise to
me." And there she stands, at the end of this rich and beautiful
book, a clear human figure making her pronouncement on life.

III   The Land's End

The Land's End (1908) falls measurably short of the high
achievement attained in other books of Hudson's essays, both
preceding and following it. Edward Thomas called it "an un-
comfortable, unsympathetic book";[25] and, while this statement
applies accurately to only a few chapters, the work as a whole
is less uniformly satisfying than its companions. It is marked by
Hudson's characteristically brilliant achievement in descriptions
of places and of the life of nature; but the earth as seen in Cornwall gave less range and variety than had the subject matter of
the greater volumes. This book recounts Hudson's earliest experience in Cornwall, which later became a favorite refuge for
him; indeed, while convalescing in Cornwall, he wrote, near the
end of his life, the beautiful pages of Far Away and Long Ago,
the autobiographical work which is clearly one of his highest
achievements.

The deficiency found in The Land's End is chiefly due to the
insertion—in the account of Hudson's actual experience—of three
long chapters midway of the volume which are primarily devoted
to generalization and speculation about the Cornish people as a
whole: "Manners and Morals," "Cornish Humour," and "The
Poetic Spirit." Hudson was always fascinated by anthropology,
though he professed no general scientific competence in that
field; and evidence of this interest appears as early as in Idle

Days in Patagonia (1893). In these chapters in *The Land's End* he is attempting to account for the qualities of the Cornish people, as he observes them, on grounds of their racial origins and their history. He is puzzled by the differences between the Cornish and the Irish; and, since he had visited Ireland briefly, the reader is inclined to wish that he had spent more time there and had written about Ireland. He might have found in the Irish people more that he could enjoy and sympathize with. He finds that the Cornish are almost totally lacking in a sense of humor. The visitor is in danger, he says, of being misunderstood if he uses figurative language of any kind in conversing with them.

Hudson's unfailing interest in children and his response to them is clearly illustrated in *The Land's End* in an incident when the children of the farm home at which he was staying brought him, in a period of extreme cold, a robin which was crippled and nearly dead. Hudson told the children that nothing could be done for the bird, that the most merciful thing was to let it fly away into the bushes where the robins sleep, and where it too would fall asleep and quickly die in its sleep. When they released the bird, "it darted away into the black bitter night"; but, in the morning, when Hudson put out the food with which he was trying to help the birds to survive the intense cold of the "great frost," he found "the wasted little cripple among them, eagerly picking up crumbs." He admits that he was "foolishly pleased" to see it there, but he comments that "a hopelessly injured and maimed bird is, like the caged bird, incapable of its proper life, and . . . is better dead."[26]

Hudson's descriptions of the ocean as seen at Land's End and from the nearby coasts are vivid and eloquent: he had seen "no such blues and greens on any other part of the British coast; and no such purples. . . ."[27] But for Hudson landscape and seascape alike were less than fully satisfying except in brief intervals "without wonderful life and the varied forms of life, which are in harmony with it, and give it a meaning and a grace and beauty and splendour not its own."[28] Foremost among the living things which gave Hudson in Cornwall the meaning and fullness of experience he craved was the common wren. He says: "Indeed, it was the prevalence of the wren which made the West Cornwall bird life seem much to me. . . ."[29] The passage which follows ranks high among all of Hudson's many characterizations of birds, and it has the advantage for many a reader of dealing with a species he has himself observed and has probably admired and enjoyed:

Not a furze clump, nor stone hedge, nor farm building, nor old ruined tin mine, nor rocky headland, but has its wren, and go where you will in this half-desert silent place you hear at intervals his sharp strident note; but not to welcome you. Your heavy footsteps have disturbed and brought him out of his hidingplace to vehemently express his astonishment and disapproval. And having done so, he vanishes back into seclusion and dismisses the fact of your existence from his busy practical little mind. He is at home, but not to you.[30]

Hudson admires and enjoys the wren most of all, he tells us, as he finds him "among the rude granite rocks of a headland, living in the roar of the sea; when the wind falls or a gleam of winter sunshine visits earth you will find him at a merry game of hide-and-seek with his mate among the crags, pausing from time to time in his chase to pour out that swift piercing lyric which you will hear a thousand times and never without surprise at its power and brilliance."[31]

Perhaps the finest and most characteristic chapter in *The Land's End* is a brief one near the end of the book, "The Furze in Its Glory." The whole chapter is a tribute to the furze: a plant not likely to be known to American readers, defined as a member of "the leguminous genus *Ulex*, esp. U. europaeus, a low, much-branched spiny shrub with yellow flowers, common on waste land in Europe" and also known, and sometimes referred to by Hudson, as gorse. The beauty of the furze depends, Hudson says, on "the character of the plant—the exceeding roughness of its spiny surface, the rude shapes it takes and its darkness, over which the winged flame-coloured blossoms are profusely sprinkled."[32]

Hudson's remarkable ability to take the reader with him, and to enable the reader to see with his eyes, is seldom so clearly evident as in this chapter:

I like to come upon a furze-patch growing on a slope, to sit below it and look up over its surface, thrown into more or less rounded forms, broken and roughened into sprays at the top, as of a sea churned by winds and cross-currents to lumpy waves, all splashed and crowned

as it were with flame-coloured froth. With a clear blue sky beyond I
do not know in all nature a spectacle to excel it in beauty.[33]

Hudson's familiar "signature," of reference to Argentina, appears in *The Land's End* as in others of his books about Britain.
In the first chapter, after picturing the streets and dwellings of
Saint Ives, the village in West Cornwall to which he first went
on his arrival in the country, he describes "the most interesting
hour of the day"—that time in the afternoon or evening when
the fishermen of the village "came lurching down the little
crooked stone streets and courts to the cove or harbour to get
the boats out for the night's fishing."[34] He is teased by a vague
association, less definite than an actual memory, of some past
experience of which this departure of the boats reminded him.
Finally, he recaptures it: the departure of the boats is like the
flight of flamingos, one by one, from a lake where they have
spent a day. This precise experience is one of those most vividly
rendered in Hudson's account of his boyhood experience in
Argentina in *Far Away and Long Ago*.

Almost a hundred pages later, when describing the farmhouse
at which Hudson was living for a time in Cornwall, where furze
and turf were burned for fuel in the "wide old open fireplace,"
Hudson is again strongly reminded of Argentina: "those primitive
cattle-breeding establishments . . . where everyone, dogs and
cats included, lived in the big smoke-blackened kitchen. . . ."[35]

The Land's End contains an interesting discussion of Charles
M. Doughty's long epic poem, *The Dawn in Britain*, and favorable comment on the writing about nature of the American,
Charles G. D. Roberts. Among other contemporary or recent
writers who are mentioned in *The Land's End* are Ruskin, Browning, Swinburne, Wilkie Collins, William James—whom Hudson
greatly admired—and Ford Madox Hueffer (Ford Madox Ford).

The last chapter of this book, entitled "Pilgrims at the Land's
End," describes the constant flow of pilgrims from all England
to this place, and it concludes with a vigorous plea for its preservation and its protection against commercial exploitation.

IV Afoot in England

Afoot in England (1909) differs markedly from the other
books of essays grouped with it, *Nature in Downland, Hampshire*

Days, and *The Land's End,* which preceded it, and *A Shepherd's Life,* which followed in 1910. It lacks the concentration of attention on a single region of England which marks these books, nor is it primarily devoted to birds and their lives as are the essay volumes of the "birds" group. As the title suggests, it gives us memorable glimpses of, or brief visits in, several parts of England—South Devon, Cornwall, the Norfolk coast, with visits to such places as Salisbury, Bath, Wells, and Stonehenge. This collection is also distinguished by wider attention to books and to reading than its companion volumes and (with the exception of *A Shepherd's Life*) to human character.

Hudson tells us in a prefatory note that about half of the material collected in *Afoot in England* had previously appeared in "various papers and periodicals." The fact that it is in large part a gathering of independent pieces, apparently unrevised, accounts for its lack of the unity of effect so marked in the other volumes of its class. *Afoot in England* does contain, however, some of Hudson's most characteristic and self-revealing writing.

Emphasis on books and writers is, as we have indicated, very marked in this volume. There is an extended passage about Mary Russell Mitford, in which Hudson tries to analyze the attraction felt by many readers (including himself) for her *Our Village,* a collection of simple stories of rural village life. Similar emphasis of space and praise are given to William Cobbett and his *Rural Rides.* It includes one of Hudson's rare comments on literary style: he declares that Cobbett's style is "The most simple, direct, and colloquial ever written."[36] He calls *Rural Rides* "a classic, and as incongruous among classics as a farmer in his smock-frock, leggings and stout boots would appear in a company of fine gentlemen in fashionable dress."[37] One whole chapter of *Afoot in England* is devoted to a writer less well known than Cobbett or Miss Mitford—Robert Bloomfield, author of *The Farmer's Boy.* Hudson tells how he had found this poem in one of the old books he bought when he first began to buy books "from an old snuffy spectacled German in a long shabby black coat"[38] at a bookstore in Buenos Aires. It develops that his enthusiasm for Bloomfield rests chiefly on the old poet's sympathy for horses, especially post horses.

We find one of Hudson's few references to Walt Whitman when he comments on a church in the middle of a forest and

far from any village, which had been built, according to tradition, as a memorial by one of William the Conqueror's lieu-
tenants who had slain there a wild boar which had killed his
child. When he quotes a local county history as stating of the
church only that it was built "for the convenience of the inhabitants of the place," he remarks: "An odd statement, seeing
that the place has every appearance of having always been
what it is, a forest, and that the inhabitants thereof are weasels,
foxes, jays and such-like, and doubtless in former days included
wolves, boars, roe-deer and stags, beings which, as Walt Whitman truly remarks, do not worry themselves about their souls."[39]

A quotation from another American writer, Herman Melville,
appears significantly in a passage in which Hudson deals more
frankly and at greater length with his personal religious attitudes
and experience than he had in any previous work. In Chapter 8,
he visits the partially excavated ruins of Roman Calleva, encounters a robin, and pictures for the reader vividly the stone
walls, "overgrown with trees and brambles and ivy." He reflects
on the centuries which have intervened since the Romans built
this city, in which "floors and foundations, with fallen stones and
tiles, were gradually buried in the soil, and what was once a
city was a dense thicket of oak and holly and thorn. Finally the
wood was cleared, and the city was a walled wheat-field—so far
as we know, the ground has been cultivated since the days of
King John."[40]

As he looks, he thinks of the people who preceded the Romans
in Britain, remarking that "the entire history of this green walled
space before me—less than twenty centuries in duration—does
not seem so very long compared with that of the huge earthen
wall I am standing on, which dates back to prehistoric times."[41]
After commenting on traces of these earlier peoples, and of the
Romans themselves and those who came after them, still to be
observed in the English people of the present, Iberian and Celt,
and Roman and Saxon and Dane, Hudson comments: "This, I
take it, is a satisfaction, a sweetness and peace to the soul in
nature, because it carries with it a sense of the continuity of the
human race, its undying vigour, its everlastingness. After all the
tempests that have overcome it, through all mutations in such
immense stretches of time, how stable it is!"[42]

But his reflection does not end there. He draws an illustration from the Argentine—of finding on the side of a ditch in the pampas some bits of ancient black pottery, made by an utterly extinct and forgotten race of men. His thought ranges to the current belief of geologists, that the cold period which exterminated Paleolithic man was a quarter of a million years ago and that there ensued "a void, a period which to the imagination seems measureless, when sun and moon and stars looked on a waste and mindless world."[43]

At this point Hudson introduces his quotation from Melville:

"It is this break in the history of the human race which amazes and daunts us, which "shadows forth the heartless voids and immensities of the universe, *and thus stabs us from behind with the thought of annihilation.*" (The italics are Hudson's)[44]

Proceeding then to comment on the feeling of painful insignificance which travelers feel in the presence of great deserts and mountains and the even greater poignance of these feelings in such regions as Tasmania, which have "no remains of antiquity, no links with the past," Hudson concludes: "I recognize and appreciate the enormous difference which human associations make in the effect produced on us by visible nature."[45]

There follows a passage which, because it is one of the few definite statements we can find anywhere in Hudson as to his religious beliefs, demands quotation in full in spite of its length:

The knowledge that my individual life is but a span, a breath; that in a little while I too must wither and mingle like one of those fallen yellow leaves with the mould, does not grieve me. I know it and yet disbelieve it; for am I not here alive, where men have inhabited for thousands of years, feeling what I now feel—their oneness with everlasting nature and the undying human family? The very soil and wet carpet of moss on which their feet were set, the standing trees and leaves, green or yellow, the raindrops, the air they breathed, the sunshine in their eyes and hearts, was part of them, not a garment, but of their very substance and spirit. Feeling this, death becomes an illusion; and the illusion that the continuous life of the species (its immortaltiy) and the individual life are one and the same is the reality and the truth.[46]

There are other important revelations of Hudson's religious thinking in *Afoot in England*. One of these occurs in a chapter entitled, significantly, "Wind, Wave and Spirit"; and in it Hudson describes his meeting with a "frail" and "timid" woman who had been a pioneer in advocating reform in the cruel treatment of animals and with substantial success. On an ensuing rarely beautiful day, "one of those rare days in which nature appears to us spiritualized," he reflects that it is possible to go beyond even those modern physicists who hold that force is the only reality, to conclude that this primal force "is but a semblance and shadow of the universal soul."[47]

But the most clearly distinguishing characteristic of *Afoot in England* is its richness in relatively fully developed portrayals of human persons. In this respect, it is the richest among the volumes of essays, with the single exception of the great book which immediately followed it, *A Shepherd's Life*. In addition to the warmly delineated characters of Miss Mitford, William Cobbett, and Robert Bloomfield as presented in the discussions of their work treated earlier in this chapter, *Afoot in England* contains no fewer than a score of vivid vignettes of people Hudson encountered in his travels. Some of these are brief, half a page or even less, but they are so sharply drawn that they live in the reader's memory. Others extend to several pages.

One of the first and certainly one of the most humorous sketches is the account of the vicar of a new church which Hudson finds in an ancient village. We first become acquainted with him as Hudson, entering the church, sees a group of small boys riotously running up and down the aisles, fighting and shouting: their noise could not be heard at all because of the thunderous roar of the organ which filled and seemed to make the whole building tremble. When the music stops, the boys instantly cease their play. Presently Hudson is aware of a man standing near him—one whose appearance and manner instantly impress and interest him—the vicar of the church. They discuss a very beautiful stained-glass window in the new church, the figure of a very handsome woman, which the vicar tells Hudson is supposed to be a portrait of the wealthy lady of the neighborhood who has contributed the money for the erection of the new edifice.

When Hudson admits that he dislikes seeing old churches torn down to be replaced by some wealthy person in his or her own honor, the young vicar assures him that in this case it was necessary. The old church was beyond repair, its floor was six feet

below the level of the surrounding ground, with constant dampness as a result. And, as a result of the dampness, the young vicar
tells Hudson, "we were haunted by toads. You smile, sir, but it
was no smiling matter for me during my first year as vicar, when
I discovered that it was the custom here to keep pet toads in
church."

Each of the best families in the parish had one, he declares,
which inhabited a hole under the family pew, and would come
up each Sunday to receive the provisions the ladies of the family
brought—"bits of meat, hard-boiled eggs chopped up, and earth-
worms, and whatever else they fancied it would like—in their
reticules. The toads, I suppose, knew when it was Sunday—
their feeding day; at all events they would crawl out of their
holes in the floor under the pews to receive their rations—and
caresses."

The young vicar confesses that the toads not only had an
unpleasant effect on his nerves, but also affected his preaching.
When the old church was about to be razed, the people were
told to remove their pets, "which they did with considerable
reluctance." The vicar doesn't know what became of them: "I
never inquired." Hudson rounds out this amazing and amusing
story with the reflection that he has had "one of the oddest incidents of my life,"[48] and he carries away with him a sense of
its strangeness.

Another full and memorable sketch of people in *Afoot in England* is that, in the third chapter, of Mrs. Flowerdew, her husband, and her children. It may be noted that Hudson rarely at-
taches names to these incidental characters; when he does, the
names tend to be clearly fictional. Mrs. Flowerdew, who has
been accustomed to rent rooms, has been dispossessed of her
furniture for her husband's debts. Upon Hudson's declaration
that they will stay anyway (his wife was with him on this
occasion), Mrs. Flowerdew brightens, borrows a bed and bed-
ding from neighbors, and is actually overjoyed to provide for her
guests.

She has four small children; and, when they heard after dark
"a call prolonged and modulated . . . far off and faint," they
"instantly went mad with excitement." "Father!" they all
screamed together. "Father's coming!" And out they rushed and
away they fled down the darkening road, exerting their four

voices in shrill answering cries.[49] The Hudsons are surprised to find that the father is "a tall, gaunt, grey-faced old man with long white hair and beard!"[50] He is a great talker, and Hudson gives a brief digest of all he tells his family about his day.

An even fuller and more dramatic account is given of a family in Surrey—intense religionists (though they treat Hudson with the utmost kindness and courtesy)—who are in deepest distress because the oldest son wants to become a user of tobacco, which they consider morally destructive if not actually sinful. One of the portraits is a reflected one, so to speak, of an old squire, dead for many years; for Hudson forms his strong impression only from what is told about him. There's a highly colorful incident of a meeting with a tramp, and there is a sharp little drama of Hudson's encounter with a waitress in Wells who refuses to serve him ale. At Salisbury, Hudson contrasts effectually two sightseers at the cathedral: one is a Scotchman who, after spending hours looking at it from the outside, refuses Hudson's invitation to go within. He declares, "it was enough for one day just to see the outside of such a building." The other is an American from Indiana who "gave two hours and a half, including the morning service, to the cathedral, inside and out. . . ."[51]

One of the chance acquaintances Hudson most enjoys—and shares his enjoyment with the reader—is a man from Australia whom he meets on a train. This man had spent his boyhood in England, then emigrated with his father's family to Australia. He has been successful there, but has always—unlike the others of his family—wanted to return to England. At last he has done so and has found he could buy the farm on which he had grown up. He is so overflowingly happy that he has to tell someone—Hudson—about it.

In sharp contrast are two memorable portrayals of young women whom Hudson met under identical circumstances in the course of his journeyings. In both cases when he is hot, tired, and thirsty from his rambles, he stops at an isolated farmhouse to ask for a glass of milk. At the first—a place notably remote and dilapidated—he is admitted and served by a young woman of conspicuous personal beauty and dignity, who waits in utter silence while he drinks. Her look he finds unforgettable—"like the look of one on whom some unimaginable disaster or some hateful disillusionment had come. . . ."[52] The second young woman

—this one with children, "five or six in number, ranging from a
boy of ten to a baby in her arms—all clean and healthy-looking,
with bright fun-loving faces"[53]—becomes happily excited when
she learns he is on his way to a village called Branscombe, which
had been her home. She tells him eagerly about it, and in her
happy excitement she puts her baby to nurse without covering
her breast until, realizing, she blushes and turns away but goes
on talking happily.

V   A Shepherd's Life

In the judgment of some of Hudson's most thoughtful and
appreciative readers, A Shepherd's Life (1910) is his finest book.
It is marked, first of all, by unity of place. Its setting is limited
almost wholly to the Salisbury Plain region of Wiltshire; and
the life portrayed—of birds, insects, trees and flowers, wild and
tame animals, and human beings—is that of this relatively limited
region. In this respect it resembles Nature in Downland, The
Land's End, and Hampshire Days. But A Shepherd's Life is
distinguished from these other highly regional books by its
emphasis—suggested by the title—on man rather than on nature.
Hudson's characterization of Caleb Bawcombe, the shepherd of
the title, is a rich, powerful, and permanent possession in memory
for any reader. It is Hudson's finest achievement in presentation
of character, not excepting those in his books of fiction.

Finally, this characterization is achieved by a complete natu-
ralness of method, a wholly unobtrusive building up of picture
upon picture and incident upon incident; A Shepherd's Life is
marked in highest measure by all the sense of informality and
person-to-person rendering of actual experience which give the
other books of Hudson's essays their warmth and charm.

The first chapter of A Shepherd's Life is devoted to a general
introduction to the region of the Wiltshire Downs—"Salisbury
Plain"—and an explanation of the fascination that this region,
above all others, held for Hudson. The chapter is enlivened by
the incident of a boy who ran a quarter of a mile across a plowed
field, carrying a gun, to the road where Hudson was passing.
The lad confesses, when questioned, that his motive in coming
to the road was "Just to see you pass." This admission leads
Hudson to reflect that the system of education current in England is all wrong for country children. Hudson then remarks

that the very emptiness and desolation of the downs, "which frightens the stranger from them, only serves to make them more fascinating to those who are intimate with and have learned to love them."[54] Hudson asserts that the purity and freshness of the air on the Downs make the colors brighter and the sounds purer and clearer than in other regions, but he also notes that he has treated "the pleasure of walking on the downs" in *Nature in Downland* and that the "theme of the present work is the life, human and other, of . . . Salisbury Plain."[55] The ultimate emphasis in *A Shepherd's Life,* as noted above, is on human characters and experience.

Chapter 2 "As I See It," is devoted to the town of Salisbury— the most important place in the world to the people of the plain, Hudson declares—supporting his assertion by vivid description of the town on market days, when the rural people gather there. His portrayals include farmers, laborers and their families, and Gypsies. With Chapter 3, "Winterbourne Bishop," Hudson focuses the reader's attention on a single village of the plain bearing that name: it is not an especially attractive village, he tells us— rather, it is notably unattractive.

With Chapter 4, "A Shepherd of the Downs," the book finally arrives at its primary subject matter. This chapter introduces Caleb Bawcombe, the old shepherd whose life gives the book its title and most of its substance. Hudson tells us that he had known him a long time and had spent many afternoons and evenings in his company listening to his anecdotes of his shepherding days. Several chapters which follow are devoted primarily to Caleb's recollections of his father, Isaac Bawcombe, also a shepherd, who was born in 1800, served as a shepherd on the same farm for fifty-five years, and lived eventually to the age of eighty-six. These memories include accounts of poaching and deer-killing on the downs, and examples of the elder Bawcombe's great strength and endurance. They include also some attention to the unbounded cruelty of the judges in rural areas early in the nineteenth century, when hanging was frequently the sentence for stealing a sheep, a matter dramatized by Hudson in the powerful short story, "An Old Thorn." Reminiscences of his father's days and experiences recur in Caleb Bawcombe's talks with Hudson throughout the volume—no doubt just as they actually came out in his conversation: the details about the cruel punishments appear chiefly in the chapter "Old Wiltshire Days" in which Caleb's and his father's recollections are interwoven.

Caleb is very fully visualized for the reader in Hudson's account of his first meeting with him in the chapter previously mentioned, "A Shepherd of the Downs." We see his long, narrow head and high forehead; his big, outstanding ears; his long, coarse, gray whiskers. Final focus of the portrait is on the eyes:

The hazel eyes were wonderfully clear, but that quality was less remarkable than the unhuman intelligence in them—fawn-like eyes that gazed steadily at you as one may gaze through the window . . . of a house at the landscape beyond. This peculiarity was a little disconcerting at first when, after making his acquaintance out of doors, I went in uninvited and sat down with him at his own fireside. The busy old wife talked of this and that, and hinted as politely as she knew how that I was in her way. To her practical, peasant mind there was no sense in my being there. "He be a stranger to we, and we be strangers to he." Caleb was silent, and his clear eyes showed neither annoyance nor pleasure but only their native wild alertness. . . .[56]

Hudson finally gains acceptance by remarking about a canary that the Bawcombes have in a cage that he does not object to seeing canaries in cages, since they are born in cages and live all their lives there, "but I considered that those who caught wild birds and kept them prisoners did not properly understand things."[11] This happened t obe Caleb's view. One of Caleb's stories of his boyhood follows, and the footing which becomes sustained and intimate is well established.

The quality of Caleb's experiences as recounted to Hudson is well illustrated by the first in the long series, which follows immediately after the meeting just described. It is a recollection of Caleb's boyhood, when, while he was out on the down one day watching his father's flock, two village boys roaming on the downs joined him as he sat on the turf. They had caught a titlark, or meadow pipit, and were quarreling as to which was its rightful owner. The dispute became so violent that it could not be settled without an actual fight, and the captive bird was put under the hat of one of the boys while they squared off. But, as the fight began, Caleb with his crook tipped the hat over, and "away flew the titlark."[57]

The boys, who had lost both the bird and a chance for a fight, threatened Caleb. But, afraid of Caleb's dog which was lying beside him, they contented themselves with cursing and threatening. Hudson comments that this "pretty little tale of a titlark was but the first of a long succession of memories of his early years, with half a century of shepherding life on the downs, which came out during our talks on many autumn and winter evenings as we sat by his kitchen fire."[58]

The texture and the quality of *A Shepherd's Life* rest ultimately on these reminiscences of Caleb Bawcombe. They are many—at least fifty by actual count, a dozen of which are recollections of his father. They vary greatly in length, from a brief paragraph to several pages, and in mood and effect from the humorous, the merely picturesque, or the melodramatic to the profoundly tragic or pathetic.

Caleb's stories are interspersed with accounts of Hudson's experiences and observations on the downs and in the forests and fields, marked by his habitual close rendering of detail; by brief historical passages about the earlier days in the region, including reference to a period of violence when threshing machines were introduced, depriving the laboring group of their accustomed income from threshing the grain with flails; and by sketches of other people whom Hudson encountered or came to know in the region.

One of the more interesting and one of the longest of Caleb's stories is that of a man with the curious name of Elijah Raven. Hudson was perhaps especially interested in this man because he discovered belatedly that he was living in the house formerly inhabited by Raven, the last of his family, and a person "of eccentric habits and of a somewhat grotesque appearance."[59] "Elijah was short of stature, broad-shouldered, with an abnormally big head and large dark eyes. They say that he never cut his hair in his life. It was abundant and curly, and grew to his shoulders, and when he was old and his great mass of hair and beard became white it was said that he resembled a gigantic white owl."[60] He lived in the house he had inherited, with a poor old man who did the cooking and housework; when the man died, he lived on alone, with "two feathered tenants, a pair of white owls—the birds he so much resembled."[61]

Elijah's one passion was for money and, through money for power: "to make himself master in the village." He hired only needy people and then at the lowest wages. He would not lend money, but he would always buy anything at all "if a poor man had to find money quickly, on account of illness or some other cause,"[64] and if he could buy cheaply enough to be sure of a profit.

Caleb Bawcombe's experience with Elijah came about because the people of the village had a small benefit society or club to which most of the farmhands in the parish belonged, the members numbering about sixty or seventy. Subscriptions were paid quarterly, but the rules were not strict, and any member could take a week or a fortnight longer to pay; "when a member fell ill he received half the amount of his wages a week from the funds in hand, and once a year they had a dinner."[63] When the secretary of this club for many years became so old and infirm that he could no longer keep the accounts, and no one could be found to fill the place, Elijah Raven astounded everybody by volunteering, and he was promptly accepted.

It was at this time that Bawcombe's collision with Elijah occurred. While engaged in dipping lambs, Caleb accidentally swallowed or inhaled a quantity of the poisonous dip and became sick. The farmer who was his employer got a doctor for him, but he was ill for six weeks. When he was able to return to work, he applied to Elijah for his half-pay from the club funds during his illness; Elijah refused him flatly on the pretext that his last subscription had not been paid. Neighbors who had also been refused by Elijah had come with Silas, but they waited outside. While Caleb was telling them of his rebuff, Elijah came out to listen; and, when Silas confronted him with an accusation of injustice, Elijah stated that he would say the same thing again if Caleb came to him again. "But if I happen some day to meet you out of doors then I'll pay you. Now go."[64] But, when Caleb did meet him out-of-doors, "the other without a word and without a pause passed by on his way."[65]

There was much discussion in the cottages, and finally one of the villagers, who was not quite so poor as most of them and who went occasionally to Salisbury, offered to consult an attorney in that city: "He would pay for the advice out of his own pocket; he wanted to know if Elijah could lawfully do such things."[66] He returned with the attorney's opinion that, if Caleb could prove in court that Elijah had made the statement about paying him if they met outside, then Elijah could be made to pay—and that he would take the case if guaranteed five pounds. The villagers raised the five pounds; and for the first time in his life Caleb saw a judge in his wig and gown and listened to lawyers. This judge was of a very different sort from those condemned by Hudson for their harsh penalties. He permitted Caleb to tell his own story:

> Then up rose Elijah Raven, and in a loud voice exclaimed, "Lord, Lord, what a sad thing it is to have to sit here and listen to this man's lies!"
> "Sit down, sir," thundered the judge; "sit down and hold your tongue, or I shall have you removed."
> Then Elijah's lawyer jumped up, and the judge told him he'd better sit down too because he knowed who the liar was in this case. "A brutal case!" he said, and that was the end, and Bawcombe got his six weeks' sick pay and expenses, and about three pounds besides, being his share of the society's funds which Elijah had been advised to distribute to the members.[67]

Wisely, Hudson presents the stories in his own characteristic easy and vivid style. Only in the final few pages of the book does he use Caleb's own language. One of these final stories, in dialect, is Caleb's only ghost story. Caleb begins, with his characteristic caution, by recognizing that many refuse to believe in ghosts because they have never seen them. He does not assert that he himself has seen ghosts, but he proceeds to relate what he did see one night as he was coming home late from his work with the sheep; it was "close on 'leven o'clock, a very quiet night, with moon sheen that made it a'most like day."[68] As he came to the stepping-stones at the ford of the stream near the village, he saw two tall women, with black gowns on, "standing face to face so close that the tops of their bonnets wur a'most touching together." He recognizes both women, "Mrs. Durk from up in the village an' Mrs. Gaarge Durk, the keeper's wife down by the copse": "But mind, I hear'd no talking when I passed 'n. An' I'd hardly got past 'n before I says, Why what a fool be I! Mrs. Durk she be dead a twelvemonth, an' I were in the churchyard an see'd her buried myself. Whatever be I thinking of?"

He turns and looks back, and he is sure of his identification: "An' I couldn't hear nothing—no talking, they were so still as two posties. Then something came over me like a tarrible coldness in the blood and down my back, an' I were afraid, and turning I runned faster than I ever runned in my life, an' never stopped—not till I got to the cottage."[69] In the last two pages of the book Hudson gives us in Caleb's dialect a story about how he once had cured a sheep of dizziness, which made her unable to walk properly, by finding and opening a swelling at the back of her head. This story is prefaced by Caleb's comment on his own life, in his own words: "Fifty years," he said, "I've been on the downs and fields, day and night, seven days a week, and I've been told that it's a poor way to spend a life, working seven days for ten or twelve, or at most thirteen shillings. But I never seen it like that; I always liked it, and I always did my best. You see, sir, I took a pride in it."[70] And the book ends with Caleb's words: "I don't say that I want to have my life again, because 'twould be sinful. We must take what is sent. But if 'twas offered to me and I was told to choose my work, I'd say, Give me my Wiltsheer Downs again and let me be a shepherd there all my life long."[71]

CHAPTER 7

Last Writings

The Book of a Naturalist and A Traveller in Little Things

TWO of the last three volumes of Hudson's essays, *The Book of a Naturalist* (1919) and *A Traveller in Little Things* (1921), may advantageously be considered together. Both are miscellaneous in subject matter, both are made up largely of articles previously contributed to periodicals; and both contain a higher incidence of light, fanciful, and amusing essays than had appeared in any previous volume. The chief external distinction between the two books is in the length of the essays. *The Book of a Naturalist* contains twenty-nine; *A Traveller in Little Things*, thirty-nine—but each has the same number of pages.

Because of their variety in subject matter and their range of treatment and tone, from the light and amusing to the deeply serious, these books afford enjoyable introduction to Hudson's essays as a whole. Hudson's chief motive in assembling these volumes for publication seems to have been his desire to increase his bequest in support of the Royal Society for the Protection of Birds: he provided in his will that after his death all income from his writings should be given to the Society.

I The Book of a Naturalist

The Book of a Naturalist is distinguished by the inclusion of four essays on serpents. Hudson had planned to write a "Book of the Serpent": but concluding, evidently, that he would never complete that project, he included these four long, thoughtful essays in the more general collection. Although Hudson's love for living things extended to serpents, he was well aware of the dangerousness of some of them. The incident of Abel's being bitten by a coral snake is one of the most dramatic in *Green*

Mansions; and the threat of the great boa, or camoodi, is realistically and symbolically employed effectively in that novel. But Hudson was wholly free from the fear and dislike of snakes, even poisonous ones, which afflict many people.

In other books, as well as in *The Book of a Naturalist,* he has appreciative accounts of adders, the venomous vipers common in some parts of England in Hudson's time; he learned how to pick up these creatures by the end of the tail and carry them around, to the consternation of observers; and he condemned the prejudice against them. The chapters on "The Serpent's Tongue," "The Serpent's Strangeness," and "The Bruised Serpent" are all marked by Hudson's attempt to gain from his readers at least a degree of sympathy and interest for the creatures so generally feared and hated; and the chapter on "The Serpent in Literature" is strikingly illustrative not only of Hudson's sympathy for serpents but also of his wide reading and perceptive evaluation of what he read.

To the student of American literature it is especially interesting to find in this essay a detailed discussion of the novel *Elsie Venner* by Oliver Wendell Holmes, of which Hudson says that it is "In prose literature the best presentation of serpent life known to me."[1] He proceeds, however, to indict the book on specific grounds. Of the hero's encounter with a huge rattlesnake in a mountain cave, when he is fascinated by the snake's eyes and would be fatally struck but for the timely intervention of the heroine, Hudson comments: "The writing is fine, but to admire it one must be unconscious of its exaggeration; or, in other words, ignorant of the serpent as it is in Nature."[2] He complains of the novel's discursiveness and points out the circumstance that, although Holmes uses a "slight sibilation in Elsie's speech" as one of the ways her resemblance to a snake is suggested, the rattlesnake—supposedly the species she resembles—"does not hiss, like some other venomous serpents that are not provided with an instrument of sound in their tails."[3]

In spite of these and other strictures, Hudson declares: "the conception of Elsie Venner is one so unique and wonderful, and so greatly moves our admiration and pity with her strange beauty, her inarticulate passion, her unspeakably sad destiny, that in spite of many and most serious faults the book must ever remain a classic in our literature, among romances a gem that has not its like, perennial in interest as Nature herself, and Nature's serpent."⁴

Of this group of essays on serpents, both "The Serpent's Tongue" and "The Serpent's Strangeness" begin with quotations from Ruskin. That introducing "The Serpent's Tongue" ends with an observation and a question: "the poor snake cannot do any manner of harm with it whatsoever; and what is *his* tongue forked for?" Hudson comments that "The passage is admirable both in form and essence; it shines even in that brilliant lecture on *Living Waves* from which it is taken, and where there are so many fine things, along with others indifferent, and a few that are bad."⁵ But Ruskin assumes that no answer is possible and Hudson then gives what he considers—and his reader is likely to accept—several very good reasons for the serpent's possession of a tongue of the kind he has.

At the beginning of the essay on "The Serpent's Strangeness" Hudson quotes some three hundred words from Ruskin's *Queen of the Air* on the emotional impressions made by snakes and on the origins of serpent myths, and he follows with other quotations supporting the view that serpents occasion powerful emotions not only of fear but also of wonder. He gives attention to the story of the serpent in the Garden of Eden: "Whether we believe with theologians that our great spiritual enemy was the real tempter, who merely made use of the serpent's form as a convenient disguise in which to approach the woman, or take without gloss the simple story as it stands in Genesis, which only says that the serpent was the most subtle of all things made and the sole cause of our undoing, the result for the creature is equally disastrous."⁶ Commenting on the story in Genesis, Hudson cites Sir Thomas Browne as shrewdly remarking that this "destructive delusion . . . hath much enlarged the opinion of their mischief."⁷

In the final essay of the "serpent" group, "The Serpent in Literature," Hudson's greatest attention—apart from the detailed analysis of Holmes's *Elsie Venner*—is given to Matthew Arnold. He observes that Arnold probably had little or no scientific knowledge of serpents. He probably knew the adder and was fascinated by its bright color and its remote and quiet life. He had sufficient sympathy and understanding to regret disturbing it and expressed his attitude in lines which Hudson quotes with approbation: "O thoughtless, why did I / Thus violate thy slumberous solitude?" Hudson also praises Arnold's poem "Cadmus and Harmonia," about a loving human couple cruelly transformed into serpents, and he proceeds to quote from it some thirty lines.

Another group of essays similarly related in subject matter, but totally different in tone and intent, is a trio about dogs: "The Little Red Dog," "Dogs in London," and "The Great Dog Superstition." As the third title suggests, Hudson does not think highly of dogs for either companionship or intelligence. Indeed, he reaches a degree of sarcasm about them not elsewhere paralleled in his writings. After a detailed account of the clean habits, affection, and intelligence displayed by a teal, he remarks that, if the teal had been domesticated, like the dog, for many centuries, and if it had been similarly petted and cherished, it would be as widely admired, enjoyed, and celebrated in books and articles as the dog. Not surprisingly, Hudson's audacity in denying that dogs are more intelligent than other animals, or make better pets, brought down upon him the wrath of multitudes of dog lovers and initiated controversy which he seemingly enjoyed.

In *The Book of a Naturalist*, the "defamatory" essay on dogs just noted is followed by an essay called "My Friend the Pig," one of the most amusing and enjoyable of the whole volume. In it Hudson boldly asserts the active intelligence of the pig—as distinctly superior to that of the dog, if given the opportunity to develop—and his capacity for friendliness and appreciation of good treatment. This essay is one of those in *The Book of a Naturalist* in which Hudson uses his experience of village and country life in England to provide a vivid, concrete, and, in this case, highly amusing background for what he wants to say.

Probably the funniest essay in the collection is another with a similar provenance: "The Heron as a Table Bird." Hudson tells how he became acquainted with two elderly, refined spinster sisters who were wholly dominated by a bachelor brother who fancied himself a sportsman and who persisted in bringing home his prey for them to cook. On one occasion he brought home a heron and demanded that it should be prepared for a special dinner. It is true that the heron—though far from edible by modern standards—had been cooked and eaten in Elizabethan times. The brother looked up directions for its preparation in old books—how long it should be hung before cooking, and how it should be prepared—and the sisters, though suffering much from the offensive odor, followed his instructions to the letter. When the time for the formal dinner had arrived and the heron was served, the brother carved generous portions for the sisters and himself and took a big mouthful. "Then something happened: a change came over his face, he turned pale, and stopped chewing; then, with mouth still full, he suddenly rose and fled from the room."[8] The sisters buried the rest of the heron in the garden and then opened all the doors and windows of the house. Late that evening the brother finally reappeared, still looking pale, and explained that he had been taking a stroll. But he never again mentioned the heron.

Included in the range of subjects in *The Book of a Naturalist* is the essay "The Strenuous Mole." Because of his small size and the fact that he is rarely seen, Hudson says, the powers of the mole as eater, drinker, sleeper, and worker are not appreciated. He comments:

It would matter a great deal if moles grew to the size of cows and bulls. In or under London they would excavate numberless tunnels which would serve as subways for the foot-passengers and for the tubular railways. This would be an advantage, but as a set-off they would, in throwing up their hills, cause a considerable amount of damage. A mole of that size could easily overturn the Royal Exchange, and even Westminster Palace would be tumbled down, burying our congregated law-givers in its ruins.[9]

Humor and satire are by no means the sole major qualities of *The Book of a Naturalist,* however. It is prevailingly thoughtful and reflective, with abundant expression of Hudson's characteristic attitudes and convictions. In the third essay on serpents, "The Bruised Serpent," Hudson expresses, for example, open defiance of Darwin by denying that fear of serpents is instinctive in any true sense. "Darwin, on the slightest evidence, affirms that monkeys display an instinctive or inherited fear of snakes," and he then observes: "To be able thus to skim with the swallow's grace and celerity over dark and possibly unfathomable questions is a very engaging accomplishment, and apparently a very popular one."[10] Hudson, who analyzes the reputed fear of snakes by horses and other warm-blooded vertebrates, concludes—at least to his own satisfaction—that this fear is not in any true sense instinctive.

It remains to validate the statement that expression of some of Hudson's most important ideas and attitudes is to be found in *The Book of a Naturalist*. His own achieved purpose throughout his essays is simply and strongly expressed in the brief essay on "Beautiful Hawk-moths" when he tells how he was able to identify a particular species from an account given by a lady who did not know a single scientific term but was able to describe with vitality the way the moth flew and hovered. Hudson proceeds to indict the authors of books on entomology, popular as well as scientific: "These writers all fail in the very thing one would imagine to be most important in books intended for such a purpose—the power to convey to the reader's mind a vivid image of the thing described."[11]

One of the last chapters of *The Book of a Naturalist*, "The Chequered Daffodil and the Glory of Wild Flowers," begins with brief accounts of Hudson's rare pleasure in finding, in some limited area, large numbers of some admired wild flower: squills, geraniums, the blue columbines. Then he turns to the wild fritillary (for which he prefers the name "chequered daffodil," using the two interchangeably) and tells how, passing a village school just when the children were returning in the afternoon, he noticed that many were carrying bunches of fritillaries, which he had considered a rare flower. He asked where they got them and returned the next day to find the spot. At first he was disappointed; the field he had been told how to find appeared to be plowed ground. Only at close approach did he realize that it was a field of fritillaries, their brownish outer petals concealing the purple spotting in the drooping bells. The rare flowers were there in thousands "and in tens and in hundreds of thousands, an island of purple on the green earth, or rather purple flecked with white, since to every hundred or more dark-spotted flowers there was one of an ivory whiteness and unspotted."[12]

Hudson then describes the fritillary flower so that the reader feels not only its beauty but also what he calls its strangeness and the sharpness of the impression it makes on the mind of the observer:

I rather incline to believe that the source of the vivid interest excited is that faculty of the mind supposed to be obsolete, but which still faintly lives in all of us, though we may be unconscious of it—a faculty which sees a hidden meaning or spirit in all strange appearance in the natural world. It is the "sense of mystery," and it is with us in sight of a magnificent and strange sunset, and of any atmospheric strangeness, down to the smallest objects that engage our attention—an insect, a flower, even our chequered daffodil of the river fields.[13]

II A Traveller in Little Things

The essays in *A Traveller in Little Things* (1921) cover, like those in *The Book of a Naturalist,* a wide range of subjects and include with frequency essays intended to give entertainment rather than to develop major ideas or express serious attitudes. The initial essay, "How I Found My Title," is a good example of the character of most of the volume. Hudson tells of sleeping at a commercial hotel at Bristol, presumably in the course of one of his expeditions as a naturalist, and of encountering at breakfast an intensely respectable-looking old gentleman, obviously highly prosperous. Assuming, after some discussion of agriculture and of conditions in rural villages, that Hudson is a commercial traveler like himself, the stranger tells Hudson that he perceives that he—Hudson—is "a traveler in little things," for sale of which he has to call on "small farmers, innkeepers, labourers and their wives," whereas he himself is "a traveler in something very large." Hudson is so pleased with this description of himself that he takes it for the title of his book.

The essays which follow include many similar brief portrayals of characters, rural and metropolitan; some of these tales are pathetic because of the circumstances described, but most are light and amusing. One of the best is "A Story of a Jackdaw," told largely in dialect. Two essays on wasps are noteworthy. In one, Hudson makes it clear that he would admire the athletically inclined young women of today, for he gives high praise to the young women who tour the countryside on the newly introduced bicycles because they are not disturbed by "A Wasp at Table." Another essay, on "Wasps and Men," carries a real surprise for the reader: the only account, so far as I have found, of Hudson's engaging in physical combat with another person

in all the range of the essays. The controversy arises when a
wasp flies into the breakfast room of a country house in which
Hudson is a guest, and begins to circle the table at which four-
teen people, mostly ladies, are seated. The ladies are alarmed,
and an athletic young man, the son of the house, declares he
will kill the wasp:

Then I too rose from my seat, for I had made a vow not to allow a
wasp to be killed unnecessarily in my presence. "Leave it to me, please,
I said, "and I'll put him out in a minute."
  "No, sit down," he returned, "I have said I'm going to kill it."
  "You shall not," I returned; and then the two of us, serviettes in
hand, went for the wasp, who got frightened and flew all round the
room, we after it. After some chasing he rose high and then made a
dash at the window. . . .

In the ensuing fracas, the young man almost captures the wasp;
but Hudson grapples with him, gets him down on a couch, and
holds him there "with my right hand on his face and my knee
on his body to keep him pressed down"[14] while he himself captures the wasp and puts it out a window.
  The same essay, "Wasps and Men," contains an account of a
young curate in the west of England, who was an ardent hunter.
Not long out of college, where he had distinguished himself
as an athlete, and established in a rural parish, he made the most
of whatever opportunity there was for competitive sports. But
tennis and even football did not satisfy him, and every day in
the week—except Sunday—he was to be seen out in fields or
woodlands, or along lanes and hedgerows, with a gun, shooting
any wild thing he could see, including birds of every kind. It
was observed that he was most notably so occupied on Mondays—
presumably as a relief from his required Sunday services and
sermon.
  On one of these occasions, while skulking along a hedge to
try to get a shot at a songbird, he had the misfortune to step
into a highly populous wasps' nest. He suffered so many stings
all over his body and absorbed so much of the wasps' venom
that he became seriously ill. The villagers opined that, being
the vigorous outdoor man he was, he would soon recover and
be the same man as before. Instead he became highly nervous
and easily alarmed, was confused when hailed by a parishioner,

and stayed largely indoors: "and the very sight and sound of a wasp in the room when he was trying to eat a little toast and marmalade filled him, thrilled him, with fantastic terrors never felt before."[15] Hudson then quotes with unexpressed but evident approval the judgment pronounced by the villagers: "Then some of the parishioners who loved animals, for there are usually one or two like that in a village, began to say that it was a 'judgment' on him, that old Mother Nature, angry at the persecution of her feathered children by this young cleric who was supposed to be a messenger of mercy, had revenged herself on him in that way using her little yellow insects as her ministers."[16]

Two of the finest essays in *A Traveller in Little Things* and in the whole range of Hudson's work as an essayist are "The Samphire Gatherer" and "Apple Blossoms and a Lost Village." The first of these, basically a simple narrative, tells of Hudson's observation from a sand hill near the coast of a woman moving on a sea-flat below, "over that damp level ground in a surprisingly swift light manner, pausing at intervals to stoop and gather something from the surface." Mystified, he decides to investigate: "Going down to her I found that she was old, with thin grey hair on an uncovered head, a lean dark face with regular features and grey eyes that were not old and looked steadily at mine, affecting me with a sudden mysterious sadness." He finds that she is gathering samphire, "of that kind that grows on the flat saltings and has a dull green leek-like fleshy leaf," which she was going "to pickle and put by for use during the year."[17] She converses with Hudson intelligently and quietly, but her eyes do not change.

After leaving the woman, Hudson tries to define for himself the impression those eyes have made on him, with their expression of profound and unrelievable melancholy. He compares himself with the painter who ignores "certain atmospheric effects in earth and water and sky" which he knows he cannot render. Confronted by such phenomena, Hudson says, a painter cultivates what is called "the sloth of the eye." He simply does not attempt to render what he knows is beyond his powers. The writer, Hudson says, faces the same problem. The most that he can do, in such cases, is to try to express and share "the emotion evoked by what he has witnessed."[18]

Hudson then speaks of the man who has formed the habit of

really looking at every face he meets and how on a London street he often encounters a face which haunts him with its suggestion of tragedy and mystery:

But it does not haunt him long; another arresting face follows, and then another, and the impressions all fade and vanish from the memory in a little while. But from time to time, at long intervals, once perhaps in a lustrum, he will encounter a face that will not cease to haunt him, whose vivid impression will not fade for years. It was a face and eyes of that kind which I met in the samphire gatherer on that cold evening; but the mystery of it is a mystery still.[19]

"Apple Blossoms and a Lost Village" is marked by an essential difference from any other essay of Hudson. The richly detailed account of his search for "a lost village" called "Clyst Hyden," of his final success and his happiness in the beauty of the place and in the goodness of the people he finds there, turns out to be a dream in a London night. This essay is noteworthy in another way for a single sentence which reveals something very deep and meaningful in Hudson's whole attitude and intention. He is trying to account for the supreme beauty which he finds in an apple tree in full bloom, and he says: "It is like nothing in earth, unless we say that, indescribable in its loveliness, it is like all other sights in nature which wake in us a sense of the supernatural."[20]

Best known of Hudson's essays in *A Traveller in Little Things*, and one of the best and best known of all his essays, is "The Return of the Chiffchaff." I am unable to find specific indication of the date at which this essay was written. Hudson had written in *British Birds* of the chiffchaff, a small brown bird, the earliest migrant to return to England in the spring. I quoted in the comment on that book his account of its song. But the style and manner of the essay in *A Traveller in Little Things* suggest much later composition. The essential emotion of the essay is grief for the recent death of a beloved friend. It seems probable, though perhaps not provable, that this essay was written shortly after Hudson had received word of the death in action, in World War I, of the brilliantly gifted young writer, Edward Thomas, for whom Hudson had a very special and intense affection.

In any case, the less than two thousand words of the essay

express what is unmistakably a poignant emotion. Hudson begins characteristically by sharing with the reader his experience "On a warm, brilliant morning in late April" as he visits a little lake he has discovered some weeks before; he finds "half the surface covered with a thick growth of bog-bean just coming into flower. The quaint three-lobed leaves, shaped like a grebe's foot, were still small, and the flower-stocks, thick as corn in a field, were crowned with pyramids of buds, cream and rosy-red like the opening dropwort clusters, and at the lowest end of the spikes were the full-blown singular, snow-white, cottony flowers."

As Hudson settles himself on "a comfortable arm-chair" in the branches of "a group of ancient, gnarled and twisted alder bushes, with trunks like trees," to enjoy the sight "of that rare unexpected loveliness,"[21] he finds himself overwhelmed by "a thought, intolerably sad, which had surprised me in that quiet solitary place."[22] He resists the feeling but fails to overcome it, even though the chiffchaffs are singing jubilantly all about him. He finds himself thinking of, and seeing in the mind's vision, friends who are gone. "They were with me, standing by me, almost as in life; and I looked from one to another, looking longest at the one who was last to go."[23] He recalls how that friend and he had walked together in this same season, with the song of the chiffchaff all about them, and how they had found together this same flower in bloom. He faces more sharply than ever before the mystery of death and the sharpness of grief for those we have loved. "Grief at their loss is just as great for those who have kept their faith as for those who have lost it," he declares; "and on account of its very poignancy it cannot endure in either case. It fades, returning in its old intensity at ever longer intervals until it ceases."[24]

Referring once more to Matthew Arnold, he declares that the poet was wrong "when he listened to the waves on Dover beach bringing the eternal notes of sadness in."[25] The essay closes with one of the most revealing and most memorable passages Hudson ever wrote:

The "naked shingles of the world" is but a mood of our transitional day; the world is just as beautiful as it ever was, and our dead as much to us as they have ever been, even when faith was at its highest. They are not wholly, irretrievably lost, even when we cease to remember them, when their images come no longer unbidden to our minds. They are present in nature: through ourselves, receiving but what we give, they have become part and parcel of it and give it an expression. As when the rain clouds disperse and the sun shines out once more, heaven and earth are filled with a chastened light, sweet to behold and very wonderful, so because of our lost ones, because of the old grief at their loss, the visible world is touched with a new light, a tenderness and grace and beauty not its own.[26]

III A Hind in Richmond Park

Hudson's last book, *A Hind in Richmond Park* (1922), is substantially different from those which immediately preceded it—indeed, from any previous work of his. Not a collection of unconnected or only partially related essays, it is a detailed, consecutive study of a single field—the senses in man and the other animals. In the publisher's announcement, preceding Hudson's death and the issuance of the book, it was given the subtitle, later dropped, *A Book of Animal Sense and Sensibility.*

I think that Hudson knew that this would be his last book. He says at one point: "I am finding it prudent on this voyage to relieve myself of a good deal of material—many bales and crates of merchandise collected in many outlandish places; otherwise this slow ancient barque, with only the wind to keep her going, will never reach port"; and this observation immediately follows a reference to a time "when I am no longer here."[27] Indeed, Hudson did not quite live to complete this final project. A prefatory note by Morley Roberts tells us that "The day before his death, Hudson told me that the last part of this book's final chapter was practically finished. All that was needed by the fragmentary script then lying scattered on his table was the thorough revision his work invariably received."[28] Hudson died in his sleep that night. The last five pages of the text carry the note that "What follows was left unarranged by the author."

The book draws its individual and attractive title from two incidents of Hudson's personal experience, both involving "a hind in Richmond Park," which are narrated at the outset. In the first, told very briefly, Hudson is feeding acorns to a doe—one of the half-tamed deer who frequent the spacious park because they have learned that they will not be molested by the human visitors to the area—when a little girl who is watching with her mother pleads to be allowed to feed the deer too. Hudson gives her an acorn on a leafy twig, and the hind accepts it, but suspiciously; and then it immediately leaps over the child's head striking backward with her sharp rear hoofs and grazing the little girl's cheeks. Too late Hudson realizes that the child is wearing a bright red jacket, and he infers that the color has angered the deer.

The second incident, which occupies several pages, tells how Hudson observes a hind lying down and chewing her cud, with her head turned toward an area of thick woods some two hundred yards away and her big funnel-shaped ears directed toward it. He realizes that she is hearing sounds from the woods, inaudible to him, and is very much interested by what they tell her of what is going on there. He seats himself against a tree some twenty yards away and tries the experiment of whistling softly. Instantly the ears are turned toward him, though the deer does not turn her head. When he keeps silent, the ears are turned toward the woods again; but they jerk back when he whistles again. Finally, the hind devotes only one ear to him, keeping the other directed toward the woods; and he learns for the first time that the two ears can be held in opposite directions:

I had not known that an animal with trumpet ears could use them in that way, receiving impressions from two sources, taken in and judged separately and simultaneously, as a bird receives sight impressions through the eyes placed (as in most birds) at the sides of the head, each with its own distinct field of vision. Or as the chameleon, with eyes mounted on rods, is able to keep one eye on the movements of an insect in its neighborhood, while the other looks at you or at some other object which attracts its attention.[29]

From these specific illustrations—of the deer's apparently instinctive dislike of red and of its capacity to hear sounds wholly inaudible to the human ear and to evaluate and be deeply interested by them—Hudson launches on his exploration of the roles of the several senses in the lives of man and other animals and on speculation about his observations. He discusses first the effect of wind on the senses and especially that of smell, theorizing that there is something which might be called a "wind sense"; from this subject, he passes to an extended discussion of the

sense of smell in general, occupying four chapters. Into this he
introduces an amusing personal experience of his on first coming
to England: his awareness of a pervasive smell in the town
where he had first landed, which disappeared when he went
into the countryside but was apparent again as soon as he returned to the town. Ultimately he discovered that "the smell of
England," as he had named it, emanated from the breweries
which he had never known in Argentina.

The discussion of the sense of smell ranges from the scent of
flowers and the observable idiosyncrasies in the human responses
to them, through observations on the world of smells which a
dog inhabits and the sense of smell in birds, to consideration of
the fact that in civilized man the sense of smell is partially
atrophied—because it is less vitally useful than to other animals—
and to the suggestion that this submerged sense may be far more
important in relation to our attitudes and conduct than we
realize.

The next four chapters are devoted to Hudson's argument for
and illustrations of a sense of direction and to the seemingly
related phenomenon of migration. He holds firmly that a real
sense of direction exists in some men both civilized and savage,
as well as in certain animals. Readers of the recently and de-
servedly popular narrative, *The Incredible Journey*, by Sheila
Burnford, will not find it hard to be convinced by the data Hudson submits in support of his view. The remainder of the book—
nearly half—is devoted to observations and speculations on the
sense of hearing and especially on the origins and development
of music and its functions, with extended attention to the music
of insects and of birds. The final chapter contains observations
and suggestions in relation to the plastic arts.

In the course of his general exploration of what Hudson suggests as a "wind sense," he ventures into the matter of telepathy
and thought transference, giving examples. Seemingly he re-
gards the evidence for "extrasensory perception" as irrefutable—
though he finds explanation for some of the examples he gives
in the exceptional acuteness of other senses. He does not hesitate
to introduce into this and other parts of the book examples of
phenomena unexplainable on grounds of present knowledge.

In outlining the general substance of idea and speculation
which gives this book its unity and its individuality in Hudson's

work, there is a danger of failing to emphasize its wealth of
concrete detail of incident and experience. If we could put the
material of *A Hind in Richmond Park* through a sieve and there-
by separate the concrete and dramatic material from the abstract
and theoretical, we would find only a very small proportion of
the latter. Hudson's procedure throughout is to utilize a wealth
of detailed, specific experience, his own and that of others, as
evidence or indication for the ideas he offers—in most cases, in a
manner that is tentative or suggestive rather than dogmatic. The
book is, therefore, exploratory and concrete rather than dogmatic
and abstract.

It is also, however, more frankly controversial than is cus-
tomarily the case with Hudson. Very early in the volume he
again takes direct issue with Darwin, about a major element in
the theory of natural selection, and he does so in strong language.
He denies that the winter whiteness of Arctic species and the
similar protective colorations of desert and forest animals are
due, as Darwin had asserted, to "gradual accumulation and inheritance of a long series of small individual variations. . . . The
insurmountable objection is and always will be that such variations are of the individual."[30] Later in the book Hudson returns
to the attack, in a comment on Darwin's suggestion that women
have more musical voices than men because "they first acquired
musical powers in order to attract the other sex." Hudson comments: "It is a passage one is sorry to read, because it was writ
by Darwin, and—it is ridiculous. . . . There was never a time in
the early history of the human species when the female courted
the male and invented song to attract him."[31]

Matching this outspokenness in relation to some of Darwin's
theories is Hudson's caustic commentary on certain other scientists and on punditry in general. Commenting on *Warfare in the
Human Body* by his good friend Morley Roberts and on the
view there developed that migrations of birds and other animals
are "negative and positive tropisms . . . enforced by light and
heat," and on Roberts' suggestion that geologists, paleontologists,
astronomers, and physicists might be called together to consider
the matter at a "round table of inquiry," Hudson comments
dryly: "These may be valuable suggestions, and I will only add
that, as those who sit at round tables are not as a rule all equally
open-minded or tolerant of other persons' opinions, it would be

well to remove any chunks of old red sandstone which may be lying about in the conference chamber before the members meet."[32]

Definitely close to sarcasm, it seems to me, is Hudson's explanation at the beginning of Chapter 8 midway in the book, of his failure to apologize for mentioning such subjects as "antipathies, pre-natal suggestion . . . even telepathy" in earlier chapters. He writes: "At present I shall only say that these are delicate and controversial subjects, also that it becomes me in treating of them to express myself with the humility proper to an amateur, practically an outsider, one who is rightly anxious not to incur the displeasure of his masters in science and psychology, and of all those who have exalted themselves to the seats of wisdom."[33]

One of the most interesting of the speculative passages in *A Hind in Richmond Park* is the one in which Hudson comments on the paucity of our knowledge of the life and experience of prehistoric man in relation to a general suggestion that such abilities as those illustrated by telepathy and thought transference may be survivals in a few of powers possessed more extensively by our remote ancestors. He writes:

how do I know what has been in the past—that dreadful past of man's history on earth? Absolutely nothing, or no more than we can know from the study of a few fossil thigh-bones and an occasional skull. And all that these tell us is that distant races . . . have been in occupation of continental areas for long periods of time, probably untold thousands of generations, and that some of these races were larger-brained than the men of the present era.[34]

Hudson, who is fascinated by the conception here suggested of Cro-Magnon man, comments: "Of their nature, their inner life, we know and can know nothing, and can only suppose that they had developed a mentality wholly unlike ours. They did not build cities of stone to live in, or, in other words, they did not create new artificial conditions of life, to be themselves remade by the conditions they had created, and were therefore not civilized in our sense."[35]

But he suggests that in Cro-Magnon man it seems possible that the savage nature had been outlived: "We are told, at all events, of one of these large-brained races, that their dentition was different from ours, that they had no canine teeth, and were not flesh but grain eaters . . . and probably had no weapons of offence and made no wars."[36] And Hudson concludes: "We cannot imagine a mentality other than our own—that of a wasp, let us say, or of a visitor from Mars; or even of a member of the human race of a subspecies nearly allied to ours, whose mental evolution has progressed so far and lasted so long as to have given him a far bigger brain than we possess, since the evolution has not been on our lines and is consequently to us unimaginable."[37]

Almost midway in the book Hudson returns briefly to the hind and to the incidents with which the book begins with a comment perhaps half-serious but one illuminated by his love of nature and all its forms and his capacity for a critical view of his own species and of human conduct. He imagines a colloquy with the hind, in which she would point out how much man had lost in "developing a bigger brain and assuming an upright posture on his hind legs." It would be, he suggests: "A great quarrel, with many keen thrusts on both sides, also some laughter, and all the time the feeling in me, bitter as death, that she had the best of the argument; that it would have been better that animal life had continued till the time of the dying of all life on the earth with no such development as that of the large-brained being who walks erect and smiling looks on heaven."[38]

In the same chapter, just preceding the imagined colloquy with the hind, Hudson restates the method and the purpose of the work in which he is engaged; "My plan then is an unplanned one," he tells us, "a picking up as I go along of a variety of questions concerning the senses, just as they rise spontaneously from what has gone before."[39] This avowed method permits him, as was previously noted, to make the book rich with anecdotes, sharp delineations of people in various moods and attitudes, and little pictures of places and brief narratives of personal experience. It also lends itself to generous use of Hudson's rich resources in reading experience. Gilbert White receives the grateful recognition accorded him in other volumes of Hudson's essays, and Thoreau, Matthew Arnold, Sir Thomas Browne and other favorites are quoted, in addition to certain strictures on poets as diverse as Elizabeth Barrett Browning and Akenside.

The most interesting of the allusive literary passages in the book is one of more than four pages, in which Hudson compares Chaucer and Shakespeare. The comparison begins with Hudson's assertion when, in commenting on the variety of pleasant fragrances to be encountered in walking along an English country lane, he declares:

The most delightful experience of this kind is when the cloud of fragrance encountered is from no flower, but from the leaf of the sweet-brier. . . . It is a fragrance pleasing to everyone, yet one would have to go far back in our literature to find its characteristic expression—even to a time when possibly the sense of smell was more acute in our race and flower-fragrances more delightful than they are to us. Shakespeare has it:
> The leaf of eglantine which not to slander
> Outsweetens not your breath.[40]

Hudson praises the lines, but declares:

However, I prefer my favourite Chaucer:

> And I, that all this pleasant sightë see,
> Thought sodainlie, I felt so sweet an aire
> Come of the eglantere, that cirtainlie.
> There is no hert, I deem, in such dispaire
> So overlaid, but it should soon have bote
> If it did once but smell that savour sote.

Or to put it in plain prose: Is there a man on earth in such despair, so overloaded with cares and maddened with anxious thoughts, who would not find instant relief and forgetfulness of all his miseries on inhaling this delicious fragrance of the sweet-briar?[41]

Hudson then declares that Shakespeare and Chaucer are for him the greatest in English poetic literature—"and one I worship and the other I love." He explains his preference as based on the feeling and attitude of the two great poets toward their characters. "Alike in their all-embracing view of humanity and power of characterisation, they are yet wide apart as East from West in spirit. . . . It was sympathy and love with insight in one [Chaucer,] and pure intellect with simulated sympathy in the other [Shakespeare]."[42]

He goes on to pay tribute to Shakespeare's great creations of character—Hamlet, Falstaff and Justice Shallow, Malvolio and Richard the Second, Romeo, Jaques, King Lear, "and many, many more. They are an immense crowd, for they have come down out of their frames or books; they are of flesh and blood, and I am walking among them as old friends and acquaintances. But where is Shakespeare all the time? I find him not, in spite of all the loud triumphant shouts of those who have discovered him in this or that character and exposed his true inwardness to the world."[43]

In contrast, Hudson says, "Chaucer revealed himself in every one of his creations, in every line he wrote. If he has a fault as an artist it is that he is too human; the sense of kinship, of brotherhood, is, however, more to me than artistry. . . . Can we in all our literature find one like him in this, a blood relation to all men, from the lowest human refuse to the highest, the kingly and the saintly?"[44]

He then declares that "All the others whose works are a joy forever are now dead—dead and gone, alas! we know it when we read them."[45] He proceeds to survey British literature swiftly— the Elizabethans, the Metaphysicals, the Classical authors, the Romantics, those he calls the "spasmodics," the Victorian giants— "Browning, cheerful in his white tie and shirt front; Tennyson, now under a cloud, sad and prophetic like the Druids of old, with beard that rests on his bosom; and last to follow, Swinburne, tattooed all over with beautiful female faces in rainbow colors, still valorously piping on his shrill everlasting pipe. Dead— dead are they all!"[46]

But if you think of Chaucer as dead you are greatly mistaken; and when you read him you need not reflect mournfully, as you would in the case of another, that he no longer treads this green earth; that he who was most alive and loved life more than all men is now lying in the coldë grave, alone withouten any companie.

I know it, because I am so often with him, walking in many a crowded thoroughfare, watching the faces of the passers-by with an enduring interest in their individual lives and characters.

But he loves Chaucer best, Hudson says, amid all rural scenes: "especially in early spring, when we together delight our souls with the sight of the glad light green of the opening oak leaves and the cold fresh wholesome smells of earth and grass and herbage. . . . Reading Wordsworth and Ruskin, nature appears

to me as a picture—it has no sound, no smell, no *feel*. In Chaucer
you have it all in its fullest expression. . . ."[47]

Even Chaucer's coarseness the—in some ways—highly Victorian Hudson is able to enjoy: "seated on a green bank, my
hand on his shoulder . . . if he falls to talking bawdy or filth, for
love of it until he makes me sick, I am a little ashamed of this
modern squeamishness, and am able to rejoice in his ranker
zest in life, his robust humour."[48] At the end of his discussion of
Chaucer, Hudson raises a question which he does not attempt to
answer: "Does he, Chaucer, speak only for himself when he
writes thus of daisies and the smalë fowlis with their melodie
and the scents of earth and leaves and flowers, or is he expressing feelings which were more common in his day than in ours?"[49]

A Hind in Richmond Park also contains the only explicit reference to his wife which I have found in Hudson's published
writings. She is mentioned as "my companion" or "a companion"
rather frequently in the earlier of the collections of essays on
nature in England, during the period when she usually or frequently accompanied him on his expeditions. The reference in
A Hind in Richmond Park occurs in a playful paragraph on
sneezes and the degree to which the sneeze and the sound it
produces differs in individuals "from the little pussy-cat puff of
sound emitted by some women to the awful outbursts of noise
in some men that would do credit to a mastodon or a behemoth."
His own sneeze, Hudson says, "shapes itself into a shrill cre-
scendo sort of yell, probably distressing to others. 'O please don't!'
was my wife's invariable exclamation when she heard it, and
I never succeeded in convincing her that it was quite natural
and involuntary. She believed it was artificial, that I had invented or rather composed it for my own amusement."[50]

Hudson's style shows no loss of variety, power, or beauty
in his final book. Though the volume is different from its fellows
in its high incidence of reflective and speculative matter, as we
have seen, and its fairly frequent intrusion of overt controversy,
it is still unmistakably and richly Hudson's in the range of material and the texture and beauty of its style. Passages notable in
this regard frequently occur in Hudson's memories of Argentina
and his boyhood there, which are numerous and often richly
elaborated in this final volume. Representative of their quality
is the final paragraph of a tribute to the upland plover, a bird

very common in Hudson's days on the pampas, and "the one I loved best." He says that these birds did not gather into flocks before migration, as many of the migrants did, and tells us he was often for weeks on horseback without ever being for a day out of sound or sight of this bird. At night during the season of migration he would lie awake for hours listening to the calls of the plovers, and remembers them vividly still: "It was the sense of mystery it conveyed which so attracted and impressed me— the mystery of that delicate, frail, beautiful being, travelling in the sky, alone, day and night, crying aloud at intervals as if moved by some powerful emotion, beating the air with its wings, its beak pointing like the needle of the compass, flying, speeding on its seven-thousand-mile flight to its nesting home in another hemisphere."[51]

CHAPTER 8

Literary Influences and Enthusiasms

I White, Thoreau, Burroughs, and Others

THERE is no difficulty at all in identifying the book which exerted the most powerful influence on W. H. Hudson as a writer. It was Gilbert White's *Natural History of Selborne*, the book brought to him from England as "just the right thing for that bird-loving boy out on the pampas."[1] Hudson tells us in *Far Away and Long Ago* that he read and reread it many times; and it is clear that enjoyment of this book and affection for its writer lasted all his life. His most extended treatment of any writer, in all his work, is the chapter called "Selborne," in *Birds and Man*. In this essay he tells of his pilgrimage to the rural village which White had made immortal, finding it unspoiled and lovely; of his visit to White's grave; and of his sense of nearness to the writer whose love of nature and living things had meant so much to him.

This reflection leads to development in Hudson's essay, more fully than in any of his other writings, of two of the most profound and pervasive of his underlying attitudes and convictions. One of these is a sense of a measure of personal immortality. As he watches the swifts and greenfinches which White too had watched at Selborne, "It began to seem to me that he who had ceased to live over a century ago . . . was, albeit dead and gone, in some mysterious way still living."[2] He permits this feeling to grow and intensify, to the point of an imagined colloquy with the long-dead writer. They discuss the famous controversy about the hibernation of swallows, and Hudson gives White some recently discovered evidence tending partially to confirm the belief that some swallows hibernate, for which White had been so much abused by later writers.

Hudson proceeds to reflect on "the marked difference in manner, perhaps in feeling, between the old and new writers on animal life and nature."[3] He recognizes acutely the difficulty of explaining or even suggesting to Gilbert White the change which has occurred within the century and more since White's death: the change which "had been rejected with scorn and bitterness by the mass of mankind at first; it had taken them years—the years of a generation—to overcome repugnance and resentment, and to accept it. . . . That anything so unforeseen had come to pass,—so important as to change the current of thought, to give to men new ideas about the unity of nature and the relation in which we stood towards the inferior creatures,—he could not understand."[4] In the imagined colloquy, Hudson has White rejecting the idea of any such change from the articulated religious basis of his own writing and has him raise the question as to why, if such a change has indeed occurred, his own book still has readers. Hudson replies, in the final paragraph of the chapter, that "the personality of the author is the principal charm of the *Letters* . . . it is a very delightful human document."[5]

Though White's *Selborne* was an initiating force in Hudson's development as a writer, the most important continuing influence —in terms of style, method, and attitude—was that of Thoreau. Judson Dodds McGehee, in his "The Nature Essay as a Literary Genre,"[6] has recognized Thoreau as the founder and primary exemplar of a new literary form in which he was followed by other writers, including Hudson. In Hudson's case, this assertion of relationship is justified; for Thoreau is quoted, or at least mentioned, in almost every volume of Hudson's later essays and always with expressed or implied approbation. Though Hudson's style is emphatically his own, his relationship to Thoreau is not limited to method and attitude in treating of nature but is also evident in his style. It is less the Thoreau of *Walden,* however, with his emphasis on ideas and social direction, of whom the reader of Hudson is reminded, than the Thoreau of *A Week on the Concord and Merrimack Rivers, The Maine Woods,* and *Cape Cod.* Here the relationships not only in style but in the whole procedure and organization of the books and the individual essays are striking.

As has been noted in a preceding chapter, Hudson ventured to challenge Darwin at the very outset of his own career, in the

Letters on the Ornithology of Buenos Aires; and he continued
to mention Darwin in volume after volume, usually in disagreement. The only naturalist-writer whom Hudson refers to frequently with approbation—other than Thoreau—is John Burroughs. Burroughs had made a study of British birds which
Hudson commended; and he seems to have approved Burroughs'
general attitude in his writing about nature.

The most surprising discovery which one makes about Hudson's reading, in a thorough study of his work, is that of its
very wide range in fields far from his own immediate interests.
Most astonishing, perhaps, is the encounter with the name of
William Langland, with quotations from *Piers Plowman,* noted
earlier. A long passage in one of Hudson's last books, as we have
seen, is devoted to expression of his enjoyment of Chaucer. A
favorite, often quoted or referred to, is Sir Thomas Browne.
Perhaps from his enjoyment of James Thomson's *Seasons,* in his
early reading in his parents' library, Hudson derived his liking
for certain minor poets who dealt with rural British life and
whom we have noted—among them Hurdis and Bloomfield.

Certain nineteenth-century writers are conspicuous in their
absence from Hudson's frequent revelations of his reading enthusiasms: the Romantic poets in general—even Wordsworth,
surprisingly; Carlyle; all the novelists; and Browning and Tennyson. Ruskin, on the other hand, is referred to repeatedly and
admiringly, chiefly on the ground of style; and Matthew Arnold
is quoted with praise, notably in *The Book of a Naturalist.*

An aspect of Hudson's life little recognized by biographers is
his active interest in contemporary literature, especially in the
last twenty years of his life. This interest, amounting actually to
involvement, is most clearly revealed in his letters to Edward
Garnett, published as *Letters from W. H. Hudson, 1901-1922* in
1923, and in his letters to Morley Roberts, collected and often
commented on by Roberts in *Men, Books and Birds* (1925):
naturally, since Garnett was a reviewer, later an influential critic
and editor, and since Roberts was also a reviewer and a prolific
writer of fiction and of books of other kinds. Both were among
Hudson's earliest and most perceptive admirers. In the one
hundred and fifty or more letters to Garnett, no less than one
hundred current books are commented on by Hudson as read
or as being read. There are extended comments on some twenty

of these, some affording the whole or nearly the whole content of a letter. The letters to Roberts give similar evidence of Hudson's constant reading of contemporary books and of his positive taste and judgments. Their friendship and active correspondence began in 1880, according to Roberts' statement in his introduction to *Men, Books and Birds;* but the earliest letters in the volume are dated 1897.

Hudson's comments on contemporary books and writers are always candid, often vigorous. Of the currently popular work of Mrs. Humphrey Ward, Hudson wrote to Garnett on May 17, 1906: "Years ago when I read *Robert Elsmere* with great labour I vowed never to choke myself with another of that woman's ill-cooked moral puddings, and I've kept my vow!"[7] Perhaps predictably, Hudson had little admiration for Henry James or for his disciple, Edith Wharton. In a letter to Garnett of December, 1913, he commented on Garnett's review of Mrs. Wharton's *The Custom of the Country;* and, when he asked Garnett to lend him the book, he added: "She appears to have followed her master and idol James in de-Americanizing herself, and to have done it even more thoroughly. Well, her picture is true: it is as rotten and contemptible a society as—ours. . . ."[8]

Hudson expressed in a letter to Garnett of November 29, 1917, his dislike of Henry James's later style—"his dear last style which he abhorred the critical world for not liking"—and stated his preference for James's early work, citing *Roderick Hudson* as an example.[9] Hudson's admiration for William James was unbounded. In a letter to Roberts of February 26, 1917, he quoted with evident satisfaction a comment on his own writing: "I remember that Prof. William James said of me that my merit was in saying exactly what was in me without any colouring from books or others and so on."[10]

One of the most interesting and self-revealing of Hudson's comments on current books by prominent writers is his lengthy analysis of Virginia Woolf's *The Voyage Out,* in his letter to Garnett of June 12, 1915:

Here are a lot of people put on a ship and when it gets to its destination they find themselves mixed up with a lot more at a hotel—all English people of one class [that of the author] all thinking, talking, and acting exactly like the people one meets every day in every London

drawingroom. All their talk—and God knows there's a lot of it—and all
they think and do has no relation to the environment—the place they
are supposed to be in which only differs from an English background
in having a sky of Rickett blue. Somewhere in S. America it is supposed to be and once or twice "natives" are mentioned. The scene might
just as well have been in some hotel on the south coast of England.[11]

The comment that Mrs. Woolf's characters wholly lack "relation
to the environment" is expressive of a cardinal standard in Hudson's judgment of fiction, one frequently expressed or implied.
No Hudson character of his own fiction, it may safely be asserted, ever lacks "relation to the environment."

The letters to Roberts are marked by Hudson's comments on
his friend's own books, which were appearing in a steady stream.
No less than sixteen of these were commented on by Hudson
within the period covered by the published letters, always candidly: sometimes with admiration and expression of his enjoyment, sometimes with definite and considered adverse judgment.
In all these letters to Roberts and in those to Garnett we see
clearly the degree of Hudson's interest in, and knowledge of,
the contemporary literary scene in England. In some cases his
range of sympathetic appreciation is surprising. Roberts comments on one of Hudson's letters (of April 12, 1906) that "Hudson, to the end of his days, was able to take an interest in the
youngest and most experimental Georgian poetry, even when it
verged on nonsense."[12]

The most notable example of this breadth of interest is perhaps Hudson's commentary previously noted, on C. M. Doughty's
long epic poem, *The Dawn in Britain*. One of his longest letters
to Roberts, that of May 10, 1906, is almost wholly devoted to
analysis of its virtues and defects, arriving at a balanced judgment. Perhaps Hudson's own interest in British prehistory, repeatedly and characteristically expressed in some of his essays,
was influential in his attitude toward Doughty's book. Hudson
was prompt to recognize the merit of Robert Frost's *North of
Boston* when it first appeared in England, calling it "a good
thing from America."[13]

Hudson was even able to praise D. H. Lawrence, though the
Victorian in him rebelled a bit. He wrote to Garnett on November 2, 1913:

I forgot to say apropos of books when I last wrote that I had just read your favorite author's *Sons and Lovers.* A very good book indeed except in that portion where he relapses into the old sty—the neck-sucking and wallowing in sweating flesh. It is like an obsession, a madness, but he may outlive it as so many other writers have done. Paul and his mother are extraordinarily vivid and live in one's mind like people one has known. Only they seem more real than most of the human beings one meets. . . .[14]

If Hudson was aware of the work of Ezra Pound and T. S. Eliot, he ignores it in these letters. Among the contemporaries most frequently mentioned are Richard Jefferies, George Gissing, and Edward Thomas. In a letter of June 27, 1918, Hudson tells Roberts that he has just been reading Gissing's *Born in Exile* "again—the third time—and find it a greater book than ever."[15] In Edward Thomas, much younger and brilliantly promising, Hudson took a deeply affectionate, almost fatherly interest, as though he had found in him the son he had never had. The last piece of writing which Hudson undertook, literally on his death-bed, was a foreword for a posthumous collection of Thomas' essays, *Cloud Castle* (1922), but Hudson died before he had completed it. In it he called Thomas "one of the most lovable human beings I have ever known."[16] Such books of Edward Thomas as *The Icknield Way, The Heart of England,* and *The South Country* show Hudson's influence clearly.

II *Significance and Contribution*

We may say justly that the ultimate theme of all literature is the life of man on the planet—with the corollary that in most literature the planet gets much less than its due share of attention. Among the most notable exceptions to the latter statement are the writer of the Psalms; Chaucer, Wordsworth, Thomas Hardy, and Joseph Conrad; in American literature, Emerson, Thoreau, Whitman, and Melville; and W. H. Hudson. Hudson, with Thoreau and Melville, met the full force of the nineteenth-century revolution in basic attitude toward the earth and man's relation to it, and they emerged with triumphant assertion of the meaning of the earth to man and of its rightful place in literature. The measure of the meaning of their achievement has not yet been fully taken.

The obviously prevailing tendency of human life in the twentieth century is toward alienation of man from the earth. Industrialism, mechanization, urbanization, accelerated travel and communication—these and other conditions mean that, for a rapidly increasing number of human beings, significant contact with the earth is increasingly limited, rare, and tenuous—or impossible. No thinking man or woman can face these facts without dismay verging on despair.

The major theme of modern literature in the Western world is the recognition of the debasement and destruction of values inherent in this alienation; and we may name James Joyce, William Faulkner, and John Steinbeck as major examples. The most depressing aspects of modern literature are those revealed by the great flood of literary production in which there is no trace of recognition or understanding of this which is happening to Western man; for what we find is merely a more or less vivid and sensational portrayal of its results.

In both England and America, however, there have been and are in the twentieth century able and articulate writers who do understand, who express their sense of loss and danger, and who reassert the values which modern man is in deadly danger of wholly losing. In England there were Hudson's younger contemporaries—Edward Thomas, Henry Williamson, Robert Gibbings—and a continuing small but clear and steady stream of writers who have dealt significantly with man's relation to the earth and its creatures; down to and including such a recent book as Gavin Maxwell's *Ring of Bright Water*. In America—so it seems to me—the literature of protest and reassertion has been richer and stronger. Certainly our greatest poets of the century, Robert Frost and Wallace Stevens, have been deeply aware of the danger of man's total and destructive alienation from the earth and have expressed their vision adequately; and a few younger poets, of whom James Hearst and Theodore Roethke are worthy examples, have done likewise.

But the strongest, clearest, and hopefully most influential body of recent American writing devoted to reassertion of the vital importance of man's relation to the earth has been in Hudson's chosen form, the personal essay; and to my mind the achievement of American writers in this field within the last thirty years is the most distinguished body of literature which that period has produced—the writings of Rachel Carson, Joseph Wood Krutch, Loren Eiseley, Edwin Way Teale, Aldo Leopold, Gustav Eckstein, E. B. White, and a goodly number of others.

I do not assert that all or any of these writers were directly influenced by Hudson's example or that they would not have written without it; but it may be indicative of relationship that Edwin Way Teale was co-author of the article first announcing the discovery of the facts concerning a significant period of Hudson's early life, his service as a collector of South American birds for the Smithsonian Institution of Washington. Moreover, Hudson is twice cited in a single representative volume of Joseph Wood Krutch, *The Twelve Seasons*. What I do maintain is the profound harmony in method and purpose between Hudson's most characteristic writings and the best of this more recent work. How Hudson would have exulted in the beauty and power of Loren Eiseley's account of being benighted in the Badlands and of hearing the voices of the migrant birds above him, in *The Immense Journey!* How deeply he would have admired and agreed with the great final chapter of Joseph Wood Krutch's *The Voice of the Desert!* How vigorously he would have endorsed Rachel Carson's powerful protest in *Silent Spring!* These writers share deeply and fully Hudson's profoundest beliefs as to the place of man on the earth and his relation to its other creatures, and they express those beliefs with beauty and power.

Notes and References

Preface

1. Ford Madox Ford, *Joseph Conrad, A Personal Remembrance* (New York, 1924), pp. 163-64.
2. *Ibid.*, p. 210.

Chapter One

1. Richard E. Haymaker, *From Pampas to Hedgerow and Downs: A Study of W. H. Hudson* (New York, 1954), p. 36.

Chapter Two

1. *Far Away and Long Ago* (New York, 1918), Everyman Edition, pp. 2, 3.
2. *Ibid.*, p. 4.
3. *Ibid.*, p. 13.
4. *Ibid.*, p. 17.
5. *Ibid.*, p. 135.
6. *Ibid.*, p. 158.
7. *Ibid.*, p. 205.
8. *Ibid.*, p. 280.
9. *Ibid.*, pp. 281-82.
10. *Ibid.*, pp. 54-55.
11. *Ibid.*, p. 48.
12. *Ibid.*, p. 67.
13. *Ibid.*, p. 194.
14. *Idem.*
15. *Ibid.*, p. 195.
16. *Ibid.*, p. 200.
17. *Ibid.*, p. 201.
18. *Ibid.*, p. 273.
19. *Ibid.*, pp. 281-82.
20. *Ibid.*, p. 286.
21. *Ibid.*, p. 288.

22. *Ibid.*, p. 289.
23. *Idem.*
24. *Idle Days in Patagonia*, Introduction, David Dewar (London, 1904), p. 104.
25. *Ibid.*, p. 109.
26. *Ibid.*, pp. 109-10.
27. *Ibid.*, p. 110.
28. *Ibid.*, p. 111.
29. *Ibid.*, p. 187.
30. *Ibid.*, p. 204.
31. *Ibid.*, pp. 210-11.
32. *Ibid.*, p. 210.
33. *Ibid.*, p. 217.

Chapter Three

1. *The Naturalist in La Plata* (New York, 1922), p. 284.
2. *Ibid.*, p. 286.
3. *Ibid.*, p. 287.
4. *Ibid.*, p. 132.
5. *Ibid.*, p. 8.
6. *Ibid.*, p. 28.
7. *Ibid.*, pp. 28-29.
8. *Ibid.*, p. 29.
9. *Letters on the Ornithology of Buenos Ayres* (Ithaca, New York, 1951), p. 60.
10. *Ibid.*, p. 55.
11. *Birds of La Plata*, p. 214.
12. *Ibid.*, p. 119.
13. *Ibid.*, p. 44.
14. *Idem.*
15. *Ibid.*, p. 52.
16. *Ibid.*, p. 55.

Chapter Four

1. *The Purple Land That England Lost* (London, 1887), p. 9.
2. *The Purple Land: Adventures in South America* (New York, 1921), p. 122.
3. *Ibid.*, p. 212.
4. *Ibid.*, pp. 298-99.
5. *Idem.*
6. *Ibid.*, p. 254.
7. Professor Keane, in the *Academy*. Hudson wrote later to Morley Roberts that this was "the first taste of praise I ever had." Morley Roberts, *W. H. Hudson: A Portrait* (New York, 1924), p. 120.

8. *The Purple Land: Adventures in South America,* p. 90.
9. In the Louise Chandler Moulton Collection, Library of Congress.
10. Lewis Mumford, *The Story of the Utopias* (New York, 1922), p. 175.
11. *Ibid.,* pp. 176-77.
12. *Letters from W. H. Hudson,* ed. Edward Garnett (New York, 1923), p. 237.
13. *Far Away and Long Ago* (London, 1923), pp. 224-25.
14. *Fan: The Story of a Young Girl's Life* (New York, 1926), p. 18.
15. *Ibid.,* p. 187.
16. *Letters from W. H. Hudson,* ed. Edward Garnett (New York, 1923), and *Men, Books and Birds,* ed. Morley Roberts (London, 1925).
17. *Tales of the Pampas* (New York, 1926), p. 1.
18. *Idem.*
19. *Ibid.,* p. 68.
20. *Ibid.,* p. 69.
21. *Idem.*
22. *Green Mansions* (New York, 1965), Bantam Pathfinder Edition, Introduction, p. xviii.
23. *Ibid.,* p. viii.
24. *Ibid.,* p. 32.
25. Hoxie N. Fairchild, "Rima's Mother," *PMLA,* LXVIII (1953), p. 357.
26. W. H. Hudson, *Letters on the Ornithology of Buenos Ayres,* ed. David R. Dewar (Ithaca, New York, 1951), p. 32.
27. *Green Mansions,* p. xi.
28. W. H. Hudson, *A Traveller in Little Things* (New York, 1921), p. 226.
29. W. H. Hudson, *A Traveller in Little Things, passim.*
30. *Ibid.,* pp. xiv-xvi.
31. *Ibid.,* p. xvii.
32. *Dead Man's Plack and An Old Thorn* (New York, 1920), p. 198.
33. *Ibid.,* 1924 edition, p. 148.
34. *Ralph Herne* (New York, 1923), p. 116.
35. *Ibid.,* p. 97.

Chapter Five

1. *Birds in London* (London, 1924), pp. 206-7.
2. *Birds and Man* (New York, 1923), p. 7.
3. *Ibid.,* pp. 42-43.
4. *Ibid.,* p. 155.
5. *Ibid.,* p. 150.

6. *Ibid.*, p. 151.
7. *Ibid.*, pp. 72-73.
8. *Ibid.*, p. 73.
9. *Ibid.*, pp. 74-75.
10. *Ibid.*, pp. 82-83.
11. *Ibid.*, pp. 84-85.
12. *Ibid.*, p. 113.
13. *Ibid.*, p. 245.
14. *Birds in Town and Village* (New York, 1920), p. v.
15. *Ibid.*, p. 33.
16. *Ibid.*, p. 34.
17. *Idem.*
18. *Ibid.*, p. 194.
19. *Ibid.*, p. 214.
20. *Ibid.*, p. 151.
21. *Ibid.*, p. 216.
22. *Ibid.*, p. 187.
23. *Ibid.*, pp. 231-32.
24. *Ibid.*, p. 232.
25. *Ibid.*, pp. 229-30.

Chapter Six

1. *Nature in Downland* (London, 1923), p. 1.
2. *Ibid.*, p. 3.
3. *Idem.*
4. *Ibid.*, p. 7.
5. *Ibid.*, p. 10.
6. *Ibid.*, p. 11.
7. *Ibid.*, p. 12.
8. *Ibid.*, p. 32.
9. *Ibid.*, p. 159.
10. *Ibid.*, pp. 160, 161.
11. *Ibid.*, p. 60.
12. *Ibid.*, p. 66.
13. *Idem.*
14. *Idem.*
15. *Hampshire Days* (London, 1923), p. 26.
16. *Ibid.*, p. 2.
17. *Ibid.*, p. 47.
18. *Idem.*
19. *Ibid.*, p. 52.
20. *Ibid.*, p. 46.
21. *Ibid.*, p. 47.
22. *Idem.*

23. *Ibid.*, p. 52.
24. *Ibid.*, p. 113.
54. *A Shepherd's Life: Impressions of the South Wiltshire Downs* (New York, 1921), p. 6.
55. *Ibid.*, p. 7.
56. *Ibid.*, p. 49.
57. *Ibid.*, p. 50.
58. *Ibid.*, p. 51.
59. *Ibid.*, p. 295.
60. *Ibid.*, pp. 296-97.
61. *Ibid.*, p. 297.
62. *Ibid.*, p. 296.
63. *Ibid.*, p. 299.
64. *Ibid.*, p. 302.
65. *Ibid.*, p. 303.
66. *Idem.*
67. *Ibid.*, p. 304.
68. *Ibid.*, p. 325.
69. *Ibid.*, p. 326.
70. *Ibid.*, p. 329.
71. *Ibid.*, p. 332.

Chapter Seven

1. *The Book of a Naturalist* (London and New York: Hodder and Stoughton, n.d.), p. 201.
2. *Ibid.*, p. 2-3.
3. *Ibid.*, p. 205.
4. *Ibid.*, pp. 205-6.
5. *Ibid.*, p. 135.
6. *Ibid.*, p. 178.
7. *Idem.*
8. *Ibid.*, p. 112.
9. *Ibid.*, pp. 225-26.
10. *Ibid.*, p. 173.
11. *Ibid.*, p. 223.
12. *Ibid.*, p. 334.
13. *Ibid.*, pp. 335-36.
14. *A Traveller in Little Things* (New York, 1921), pp. 282-83.
15. *Ibid.*, p. 291.
16. *Ibid.*, p. 292.
17. *Ibid.*, pp. 82-83.
18. *Ibid.*, p. 88.
19. *Ibid.*, p. 89.
20. *Ibid.*, pp. 130-31.

22. *Ibid.*, pp. 263-64.
23. *Ibid.*, p. 288.
24. *Ibid.*, p. 270.
25. *Ibid.*, p. 271.
26. *Ibid.*, pp. 271-72.
27. *A Hind in Richmond Park* (New York, 1923), p. 43.
28. *Ibid.*, p. v.
29. *Ibid.*, p. 8.
30. *Ibid.*, p. 31.
31. *Ibid.*, pp. 233-34.
32. *Ibid.*, pp. 146-47.
33. *Ibid.*, pp. 103-4.
34. *Ibid.*, pp. 46-47.
35. *Ibid.*, p. 47.
36. *Idem.*
37. *Idem.*
38. *Ibid.*, p. 121.
39. *Ibid.*, p. 119.
40. *Ibid.*, pp. 62-63.
41. *Ibid.*, p. 63.
42. *Ibid.*, p. 64.
43. *Ibid.*, pp. 64-65.
44. *Ibid.*, p. 65.
45. *Idem.*
46. *Ibid.*, pp. 65-66.
47. *Ibid.*, p. 66.
48. *Ibid.*, p. 67.
49. *Idem.*
50. *Ibid.*, pp. 203-4.
51. *Ibid.*, p. 160.

Chapter Eight

1. *Far Away and Long Ago* (New York, 1918), p. 323.
2. *Birds and Man* (New York, 1923), p. 247.
3. *Ibid.*, p. 251.
4. *Ibid.*, pp. 254-55.
5. *Ibid.*, p. 257.
6. *Dissertation Abstracts*, XIX, pp. 1388-89.
7. Edward Garnett, ed., *Letters from W. H. Hudson* (New York, 1923), p. 112.
8. *Ibid.*, p. 183.
9. *Ibid.*, p. 242.
10. Morley Roberts, ed., *Men, Books and Birds* (London, 1925), p. 122.

11. Garnett, *op. cit.*, p. 203.
12. Roberts, *op. cit.*, p. 62.
13. *Ibid.*, p. 113.
14. Garnett, *op. cit.*, p. 181.
15. Roberts, *op. cit.*, p. 214.
16. Edward Thomas, *Cloud Castle* (London, 1922), p. v.

Selected Bibliography

PRIMARY SOURCES

Since the books of W. H. Hudson are listed in the Chronology, with dates of first publication, the following listing is alphabetical. Only the editions quoted in the text are specified.

1. BOOKS

Adventures Among Birds. New York: E. P. Dutton & Co., 1920.
Afoot in England. New York: Alfred A. Knopf, Inc., 1933.
Birds and Man. New York: Alfred A. Knopf, Inc., 1923.
Birds in London. New York: E. P. Dutton & Co., 1923.
Birds of La Plata. New York: E. P. Dutton & Co., 1920.
The Book of a Naturalist. New York: E. P. Dutton & Co., 1923.
British Birds. London: Longmans, Green & Co., 1895.
A Crystal Age. New York: E. P. Dutton & Co., 1917.
Dead Man's Plack and An Old Thorn. New York: E. P. Dutton & Co., 1920.
Fan: The Story of a Young Girl's Life. New York: E. P. Dutton & Co., 1926.
Far Away and Long Ago. New York: Everyman Edition, 1918.
Gauchos of the Pampas and Their Horses. Hanover, New Hampshire. Westholm Publications, 1963. Contains Hudson's stories, "The Story of a Piebald Horse" and "Cristiano: The Sentinel Horse."
Green Mansions. New York: Bantam Pathfinder Ed., 1965.
Hampshire Days. New York: E. P. Dutton & Co., 1923.
A Hind in Richmond Park. New York: E. P. Dutton & Co., 1923.
Idle Days in Patagonia. New York: E. P. Dutton & Co., 1923.
The Land's End. New York: Alfred A. Knopf, Inc., 1926.
A Little Boy Lost. London: Duckworth & Co., 1920.
The Naturalist in La Plata. New York: E. P. Dutton & Co., 1922.
Nature in Downland. New York: E. P. Dutton & o., 1923.
The Purple Land. London: Sampson Low, 1887.

Ralph Herne. New York, Alfred A. Knopf, Inc., 1923.

A Shepherd's Life. New York: E. P. Dutton & Co., 1921.

A Traveller in Little Things. New York: E. P. Dutton & Co., 1921.

WEST, HERBERT FAULKNER. *For a Hudson Biographer.* Iowa City, Iowa: Prairie Press, 1958. Contains the text of Hudson's will.

2. ANTHOLOGIES

The Best of W. H. Hudson. Edited by Odell Shepard. New York: E. P. Dutton & Co., 1949.

A Hudson Anthology. Edited by Edward Garnett. New York: E. P. Dutton & Co., 1924.

3. LETTERS, ETC.

Letters from W. H. Hudson, 1901-1922. Edited by Edward Garnett. New York: E. P. Dutton & Co., 1923.

Men, Books and Birds. Edited by Morley Roberts. London: Jonathan Cape, Travellers Library, 1928.

W. H. Hudson's Letters to R. B. Cunninghame-Graham. Edited by Richard Curle. London, Golden Cockerel Press, 1941.

Letters on the Ornithology of Buenos Ayres. Ithaca, N.Y.: Cornell University Press, 1951.

Two Letters on an Albatross. W. H. Hudson and R. B. Cunninghame-Graham. Introd. Herbert Faulkner West. Hanover, New Hampshire: Westholm Publications, 1955.

William Henry Hudson's Diary Concerning His Voyage from Buenos Aires to Southampton on the Ebro: Written to His Brother, Albert Merriam Hudson. With Notes by Dr. Jorge Cesares. Hanover, New Hampshire: Westholm Publications, 1958.

Preface, Paul Fountain, *The Great Deserts and Forests of North America.* London: Longmans, Green & Co., 1901.

SECONDARY SOURCES

1. BIOGRAPHIES AND CRITICAL STUDIES

DOBIE, J. FRANK. Foreword, *Gauchos of the Pampas and Their Horses.* Hanover, New Hampshire: Westholm Publications, 1963. Compares the treatment of gaucho life and character in the writings of Cunninghame-Graham and Hudson, with strong preference for the latter.

GODDARD, HAROLD. *W. H. Hudson, Bird-Man.* New York: E. P. Dutton & Co., 1928. Brief and superficial.

HAMILTON, ROBERT. *W. H. Hudson: The Vision of Earth.* London: J. M. Dent & Sons, 1946. Appreciative study.

HAYMAKER, RICHARD E. *From Pampas to Hedgerows and Downs: A Study of W. H. Hudson.* New York: Bookman Associates, 1954. Most thorough study of Hudson's writings thus far.

ROBERTS, MORLEY. *W. H. Hudson: A Portrait.* London, E. P. Dutton & Co., 1924. Highly personal and illuminating; the record of Hudson's longest and most intimate literary friendship.

TOMALIN, RUTH. *W. H. Hudson.* London; H. F. & G. Witherby Ltd., 1954. Most recent and dependable biography.

2. ESSAYS AND BOOKS CONTAINING REFERENCES TO HUDSON

CANBY, HENRY SEIDEL. *Definitions.* Second Series. New York: Harcourt, Brace & Co., 1924. Positive, discriminating comment. Canby sees Hudson's as an important voice in the protest against industrialism and commercialism.

CONRAD, JOSEPH. *Last Essays.* New York: Doubleday & Co., 1926. Brief but positive tribute of appreciation.

CUTRIGHT, PAUL RUSSELL. *The Great Naturalists Explore South America.* New York: Macmillan, 1940. Recognizes the importance of Hudson's scientific contributions.

DE LA MARE, WALTER. *Pleasures and Speculations.* London: Faber & Faber, 1940. Warmly appreciative general comment on Hudson's achievement as a writer.

FORD, FORD MADOX. *Portraits from Life.* Boston and New York: Houghton Mifflin Co., 1937. Marked by Ford's characteristic informality and extreme statements; deeply appreciative.

————. *Thus to Revisit.* New York: Octagon Books, 1966. First published, 1921. ". . . the unapproached master of the English tongue."

GALSWORTHY, JOHN. *Candelabra.* New York: Charles Scribner's Sons, 1933. Treats Hudson's fiction only; objective but appreciative.

GORMAN, HERBERT. *Procession of Masks.* Boston: Brimmer, 1923. Superficial and inadequate.

HIND, C. LEWIS. *More Authors and I.* London: John Lane, 1922. Approving brief comment.

JAMES, WILLIAM. *Talks to Teachers and Students.* New York: Henry Holt & Co., 1900. ". . . a man who *can* write . . . this admirable author."

MASSINGHAM, H. J. *Untrodden Ways.* New York: E. P. Dutton & Co., 1933. Detailed and discerning discussion, by one who knew Hudson personally.

MUMFORD, LEWIS. *The Story of the Utopias.* New York: Boni and Liveright, 1922. On *A Crystal Age* only.

REID, FORREST. *Retrospective Adventures.* London: Faber & Faber, 1941. One of the best general comments on Hudson's writings, thorough and discerning.

THOMAS, EDWARD. *A Literary Pilgrim in England.* New York: Dodd, Mead & Co., 1917. Tribute from a younger writer whom Hudson

especially admired and encouraged; somewhat formal and consciously restrained.

3. PERIODICALS

BAKER, CARLOS H. "The Source-book for Hudson's *Green Mansions*."
Publications of the Modern Language Association, LXI (March,
1946), 252-57. Suggests Lady Morgan's *The Missionary* (1811).

COLTON, A. "The Quality of W. H. Hudson." Brief but penetrating
comment. *Yale Review*, n.s. VI (July, 1917), 856-58.

CURLE, RICHARD. "W. H. Hudson." *Fortnightly Review*, CXVIII
(October, 1922), 602-19. Thoughtful, discerning tribute published shortly after Hudson's death.

DEWAR, DAVID R. "W. H. Hudson's First Days in England." *Notes
and Queries*, n.s. VI (February, 1959), 57-58. New information
on Hudson's activities immediately after his arrival in England
from Argentina.

———. "W. H. Hudson's Visit to Ireland." *Notes and Queries*, n.s.
VIII (May, 1960), 188. Shows that Hudson probably made a
short visit to Ireland during his early years in England.

FAIRCHILD, HOXIE. "Rima's Mother." *Publications of the Modern
Language Association*, LXVIII (June, 1953), 365-70. Adverse
comment on *Green Mansions*, suggesting as a possible source
Songs of a Worker, by Arthur O'Shaughnessy, 1881.

FLETCHER, J. V. "The Creator of Rima, W. H. Hudson: A Belated
Romantic." *Sewanee Review*, XLI (January, 1933), 24-40. Careful, appreciative general discussion of Hudson's achievement as a
writer.

FORD, FORD MADOX (FORD MADOX HUEFFER). "William Henry Hudson: Some Reminiscences." *Little Review*, VII (May-June, 1920),
1-12. This and the two following articles, marked by Ford's
characteristic informality and vigor, express profound respect,
active appreciation.

———. "Three Americans and a Pole." *Scribner's Magazine*, XC
(October, 1931), 379-386.

———. "William Henry Hudson." *American Mercury*, XXXVII
(March, 1936), 306-17.

GARNETT, EDWARD. "William Henry Hudson: An Appreciation." *The
Academy and Literature*, LXII (June 21, 1902), 632-34. This
and the two following items express both personal admiration
from one who knew Hudson, and objective critical analysis and
judgment.

———. "William Henry Hudson." *Dial*, LXII (February 8, 1917),
83-87.

_____. "The Genius of W. H. Hudson." *Literary Digest International Book Review*, I (December, 1922), 23, 77-79.

HAMILTON, ROBERT. "The Spirit of W. H. Hudson: An Evaluation." *Quarterly Review*, CCLXXV (October, 1940), 239-48. Generally sound and thoughtful comment.

HARPER, GEORGE McLEAN. "Hardy, Hudson, Housman." *Scribner's Magazine*, LXXIII (August, 1925). Considers the relation of Hudson's work to that of two great contemporaries.

HUGHES, MERRITT Y. "A Great Skeptic: W. H. Hudson." *University of California Chronicle*. XXVI (April, 1924) 161-74. Lengthy analysis; admiring but unsound in general conclusions as to Hudson's religious views.

HUNT, VIOLET. "Death of Hudson." *English Review*, XXXVI (January, 1923), 23-35. Extremely detailed firsthand account of the circumstances of Hudson's death and funeral.

LANDRY, RUDOLPH J. "The Source of the Name 'Rima' in *Green Mansions*." *Notes and Queries*, n.s. III (December, 1956), 545-46.

POUND, EZRA. "Hudson: Poet Strayed into Science." *Little Review*, VII (May-June, 1920) 13-17. Marked by Pound's characteristic vigor and inaccuracy.

RHYS, ERNEST. "W. H. Hudson, Rare Traveller." *Nineteenth Century*, LXXXVIII (July, 1920), 72-78. Discerning recognition of the personal qualities of Hudson's writings.

RODKER, JOHN. "W. H. Hudson." *Little Review*, VII (May-June, 1920), 18-28. Penetrating, thoughtful appraisal.

SALT, HENRY S. "William Henry Hudson, As I Saw Him." *Fortnightly Review*, CXIX (February, 1926), 214-24. Personal reminiscence marked by insight and positive value.

TEALE, EDWIN WAY, AND WASSON, R. GORDON. "W. H. Hudson's Lost Years," *Saturday Review of Literature*, XX (No. 15), 15-17. Reports discovery of records of Hudson's collecting bird skins for the Smithsonian Institution, during his early years before leaving Argentina.

Index

(The works of W. H. Hudson are listed under his name)